BE the FINAL CURTAIN

What happens when we die

RICHARD ROE

Zaccmedia

Published by Zaccmedia
www.zaccmedia.com
info@zaccmedia.com

Published December 2014

Unless otherwise stated, all Scripture quotations are taken from the
Revised Standard Version Bible (RSV). Copyright © 1946, 1952, 1971
(the Apocrypha is copyrighted 1957, 1977) by the Division of Christian
Education of the National Council of the Churches of Christ in the USA.

ISBN: 978-1-909824-55-3

British Library Cataloguing-in-Publication Data
A catalogue record for this book is available from the British Library.

Zaccmedia aims to produce books that will help to extend and build
up the Kingdom of God. We do not necessarily agree with every view
expressed by the authors, or with every interpretation of Scripture
expressed. We expect readers to make their own judgment in the light
of their understanding of God's Word and in an attitude of Christian
love and fellowship.

Contents

Foreword

Many go through life without the slightest thought about the most foundational and important questions in life – where did I come from, why am I here, how do I decide right and wrong and what happens after I die? I think it was Socrates who said that the unexamined life was not worth living. He would have been bemused by the fact that, not-withstanding the explosion in the amount of knowledge available to humans in the 21st century, the answers to these questions for many are often, at best, murky.

Richard has done us a favour by writing this book. This book points us in the direction where we can find answers to these questions that both accord with our reason and our experience, and correspond to reality. He has reminded us how important it is to start with the end in mind.

Indeed, many believe that death is the end. The suicide rate in the UK is about 20 per day. This number excludes many who would have attempted or contemplated suicide.

But what if the end was not death? What if death was merely a portal through which we pass through either into the eternal loving presence of our Maker or into his wrathful judgment?

Some may think that starting a book with a funeral is a morbid way of beginning. But it is in understanding death that we learn to live. The psalmist says in Psalm 39v4:

'Lord, let me know my end,
and what is the measure of my days;
let me know how fleeting my life is!'

Many people I know tend to work better under the pressure of deadlines. In a sense, that is understandable. Our minds are a lot more focused about what is important when there is a deadline for a project looming. The psalmist is telling us, "Wouldn't that be the same with life?"

Richard is someone who is well-placed to remind us of that final deadline when we have to stand before our Maker to give an account of how we have lived our lives. Richard is keen that all will be able to meet that deadline with the confidence that they will find favour with God through the atoning blood of Christ. His sense of urgency is an inspiration.

I count it a privilege to know Richard, and I warmly commend this book to those who may be seeking an answer to life's questions or may know of someone who is seeking.

Roger Ong
Assistant Minister
St John's Church, Downshire Hill
Hampstead, London

Our Precious Heritage

On a hill outside North Nibley in Gloucestershire stands a monument to William Tyndale who translated the Bible into English so that even a ploughboy could understand the scriptures. This man risked his very life to do that work. He was born in 1494 and died in 1536. He was put to death because he had translated the Bible into English. This is why Tyndale is revered by Christians. We may find it strange that such an action was illegal in those days. Most of us have a copy of the Bible on our bookshelves and are privileged to have the opportunity to read this book in our own language. The Bible has been translated into many languages so that others too may read it in their mother tongue. Translation is a painstaking work, and those of us who have the Bible in our own language are blessed if we read it. However, most people in this country have yet to benefit from this holy book because we do not read it. Why might this be? A number of reasons come to mind:

- We think it is 'religious', so it is only for the professional clergy;
- We have preconceived ideas as to what it might say;
- We have been told that it is a work of poetry to be admired, and no more;
- We procrastinate, saying 'I am interested, and I will read it when I have the time';
- We reckon that if we take it seriously we will no longer be god of our own lives;
- We do not know how relevant it is to our lives.

This book is written to change your mind on these misunderstandings, and to show you that in the Bible there is some really good news for you. The Bible was written to assure us that we can have eternal life, and can be sure of going to heaven when we die.

> *I write this to you who believe in the name of the Son of God, that you may know that you have eternal life (1 John 5v13).*

That is the best news you'll ever hear. You may wonder, rightly, how this can be. It will become clearer as you read on. However, the Bible is not only a book containing good news. It also contains dire warnings regarding where we might spend eternity. Indeed, God will judge us by his Word, the Bible. We should not spurn such warnings. They are a mercy to us given by a loving God who desires that all men be saved, meaning rescued from eternal damnation (2 Peter 3v9).

When Paul was called upon to defend himself at a trial before King Agrippa his aim was not to put up a legal defence of himself but, rather, to take the opportunity to present the good news of Jesus Christ to King Agrippa and the rest of those present, that they might all become Christians like him: ... *Agrippa said to Paul, 'In a short time you think to make me a Christian!' And Paul said, 'Whether short or long, I would to God that not only you but also all who hear me this day might become such as I am ...' (Acts 26v28–29).*

That, in a nutshell, is my aim in writing this book: to make the good news of the Bible so plain that you come to believe, and receive from God his promised gift of eternal life. This simple good news has been obscured. We could be robbed of our inheritance by mockers and belittlers who put us off examining the truth for ourselves. We don't have an inherent right to have the truth handed to us on a plate. We have a mind of our own and we need to apply it. We must not let the mockers cheat us out of heaven so that we go to hell by default.

Please read the following chapters with an open heart and mind. Ask the living God, your heavenly Father, to speak to you. He loves you and wants the best for you. The living God will make the truth clear to you if you ask him. *He who planted the ear, does he not hear? He who formed the eye, does he not see? (Psalm 94v9).* He will hear your questions and answer you. Study the Bible to see if it agrees with what you read here: *Now these Jews were more noble than those in Thessalonica, for they received the word with all eagerness, examining the scriptures daily to see if these things were so (Acts 17v11).* They heard Paul's teaching and verified it against scripture.

The best way for us to honour those who have dedicated their lives to translating the Bible is to take time to read it. The following chapters will look at various passages of scripture with the aim of bringing you to faith in Christ. However, I cannot convert you. Only God can do that. This is why it is futile for countries to legislate against conversion to Christianity. It is a waste of time and effort. No one can stop God's purposes!

I hope that you will develop a love for God's Word, as Jeremiah did. God's words became a joy to him: *Thy words were found, and I ate them, and thy words became to me a joy and the delight of my heart ... (Jeremiah 15v16).*

It is vital that we do not put off reading the Bible and seeking God. We do not know how long we will live. Consider 9/11, and the Japanese earthquake and tsunami of 2011. What if we had been in the wrong place? What if we had been in Japan the moment the devastating tidal wave struck, and were swept to our deaths? What if we had been in the New York Twin Towers on that terrible day when the aeroplanes were flown into them?

We are given personal reminders of death when a relative, friend or colleague dies. The regular funeral processions through our streets are also sobering reminders, and much-needed ones, of our short and passing lives. Occasions of mourning are not pleasant but they do give us a reality check on the brevity of our lives, whereas occasions of feasting, though enjoyable, tend to blot out any thoughts of death, at least for the moment.

> *It is better to go to the house of mourning than to go to the house of feasting; for this is the end of all men, and the living will lay it to heart (Ecclesiastes 7v2).*

We do not honour God's Word by merely placing it on a pedestal. We honour the Bible by reading it, trusting it, and then responding to it. If we place our faith in the promise of God, our sins are pardoned and we receive eternal life as a gift. When we receive such amazing grace from God we will want to serve him, not from coercion but from gratitude. *But God shows his love for us in that while we were yet sinners Christ died for us (Romans 5v8).*

In this book I have used several quotes from the Bible. You may have a limited knowledge, or none, of the Bible. The references are provided to enable you to look up these passages should you wish to do so. Alternatively, you may read the book straight through. If you become a Christian, or you wish to study the Bible for yourself, the scripture quotes and references will be useful.

The Bible is made up of sixty-six books which are divided into chapters and verses. For example, Romans 5v8 refers to the book of Romans, chapter 5 verse 8.

There are many references to Jesus in this book. Sometimes I may refer to him as *Jesus Christ* or *Christ,* and at other times I may refer to him as *Jesus.* I may also refer to him as *Jesus of Nazareth.* Nazareth was the place where Jesus grew up. No significance should be placed on how I refer to him in these pages. However, to assist the reader, I will provide a brief explanation for the different names. *Christ* is his title, and means God's anointed or chosen king. *Jesus* is the name given to him by the angel who appeared to Joseph, and means Saviour, *for he will save his people from their sins (Matthew 1v21).*

A brief mention of 'the Trinity' is perhaps called for. This Christian doctrine explains what is written in the Bible.

Essentially the Bible refers to God the Father, God the Son and God the Holy Spirit. For example, Mark 1v9–11 refers to all three persons of the Trinity: *In those days Jesus came from Nazareth of Galilee and was baptized by John in the Jordan. And when he came up out of the water, immediately he saw the heavens opened and the Spirit descending upon him like a dove; and a voice came from heaven, 'Thou art my beloved Son; with thee I am well pleased.'*

The Father, Son and Holy Spirit are also referred to as the three persons of 'the Godhead'. It is not within the scope of this book to go into detail about the Trinity, but it is mentioned here so that you will understand the Christian terminology used throughout the book.

As we consider our subject, I hope that those of us who have been privileged to read the Bible in our own language will discover just how precious our heritage is – and will want to share it with others.

We will begin by considering funerals, and why they are of great importance to us.

The Funeral Cortège

The other day I saw a horse-drawn hearse moving sedately along the road. My attention was first awakened by the sound of the clip-clop of the horseshoes on the tarmac reverberating up the road.

As it approached me I observed a beautiful array of floral wreaths that bedecked the hearse, and I began to consider what I saw. Here was a glorious triumphal exit for a body about to go to the grave or be incinerated. I thought on how the human casket, which once entombed a living soul, was now empty. The soul had gone for his or her reckoning before Almighty God. Yet, as I pondered this still further, it seemed to me a wonderful timely reminder to all it passed by, that death will be coming for each of us one day. We too are on death row. There is no escape. Surely this sombre but colourful cortège is a timely procession of witness to the death that awaits us all.

So we are warned time and again to get right with God now. Tomorrow may be too late! A nuisance, this funeral procession, holding up the cars in busy traffic, blocking their paths. They want to get on with their own business, but the traffic is moving to the slow tempo of the hearse ahead.

A nuisance? I think not.

A kind service has been done for us all.

We, all of us, will die.

I saw a sermon preached today. I heard it loud and clear.

I saw a sermon pass along the road with stately grandeur.

The pleasantries, the eulogies, and the platitudes uttered at the funeral service did nothing, but that stately horse and cart said it all.

So let us pay careful attention. A great sermon was preached that day by the passing horse and cart!

Then I saw and considered it; I looked and received instruction (Proverbs 24v32).

Chapter One

It's Your
Own Funeral

You may find this a rather odd title for the first chapter, but let me explain. I have been to several funerals over the years, mainly those of relatives. I remember attending my grandfather's funeral many years ago and wondering how I would like my own to be conducted. Some people leave precise instructions in their wills. Some even address the attendees by means of a pre-recorded video or a written message.

This may seem fanciful, but just suppose you could attend your own funeral. What would you say to the people there? How would you want it conducted? What music would you choose?

First, we have to ask: 'What is the purpose of a funeral?' These events occur every day, but few affect us personally. They are times of grief as we remember the passing of a loved one, friend, neighbour or colleague.

For the Christian they can also be times of rejoicing, for although we feel sorrow at knowing we cannot enjoy their company any more in this life, we are glad to know that they have gone to heaven. We need not 'grieve' like people 'who have no hope'.

> *But we would not have you ignorant, brethren, concerning those who are asleep, that you may not grieve as others do who have no hope (1 Thessalonians 4v13).*

Funerals provide us with the opportunity for the following:

- To comfort the bereaved;
- To bring the bereaved before God in prayer;
- To remember and honour the dead;
- To thank God for the life of the dead person;
- To remind us that we are mortal: one day we will die too;
- To humble ourselves before God who created all life;
- To show people how they can go to heaven and avoid hell when they die;
- To glorify God.

When my father died in 1993 I was taken aback by the extent of my grief. My grief was heightened by the grief of others around me. It is right to mourn, but we should also thank God that we have been able to share in that person's life. It is difficult to be thankful while we are mourning, but the psalmist says: *He who brings thanksgiving as his sacrifice honours me (Psalms 50v23).* We chose this verse as the theme for my father's funeral.

The book of Ecclesiastes tells us that the key purpose of a funeral is to remind us of our mortality. We are all destined to die, but we usually put this thought out of our minds.

It is better to go to the house of mourning than to go to the house of feasting; for this is the end of all men, and the living will lay it to heart (Ecclesiastes 7v2).

Having said all this, let us imagine conducting our own funeral. Let us assume it follows the usual Church of England pattern of hymns, Bible readings, prayers, and a short 'eulogy' from the vicar praising the person who has died.

There you are, the deceased, present in person, watching and listening. The eulogy might make you squirm with embarrassment. It is very interesting to those gathered, who may hear amazing things about you they never knew.

Sadly, and strangely, we take one another for granted during life, and only realise someone's worth when they pass away. We often fail to tell people how much we appreciate them when they are alive. A beautiful poem by Derek Bingham brings this point home forcefully:

If with pleasure you are viewing
Any work a man is doing,
If you like him or you love him, tell him now.
Don't withhold your approbation,
Till the parson makes oration
And he lies with snow-white lilies on his brow.
For no matter how you shout it,
He won't really care about it,
He won't know how many teardrops you have shed.
If you think some praise is due him, now's the time
to slip it to him,

For he cannot read his tomb stone when he's dead.
More than fame and more than money
Is the comment kind and sunny,
And the hearty warm approval of a friend.
For it gives to life a savour,
And it makes you stronger, braver,
And it gives you heart and spirit to the end.
If he earns your praise – bestow it.
If you like him, let him know it.
Let the words of true encouragement be said.
Do not wait till life is over
And he's underneath the clover;
For he cannot read his tombstone when he's dead.

(This poem is adapted from Derek Bingham's book *Encouragement, the Oxygen Of The Soul,* Christian Focus Publications, 1997).

You may follow a different religion. Perhaps you are a Hindu or a Buddhist, a Muslim or a Jew. You may be a lapsed churchgoer, or nominal in your religious beliefs. Perhaps you belong to a group such as the Mormons or Jehovah's Witnesses. Whatever our beliefs and whatever group we belong to, we are all going to die. Whether rich or poor, wise or foolish, we have this in common: we all die and leave whatever possessions we have to others (Psalm 49). Therefore it is worth taking time to consider what the Bible says about death, and life after death.

We will return to the fantasy of conducting our own funeral in the final chapter. However, we first need to consider the question of why we die. This will be the subject of the next chapter.

Chapter Two

The Origin of Death, or Why We Die

THE CERTAINTY OF DEATH

Clearly, a book considering funerals presupposes death. It seems appropriate that we should consider the matter of death. Death is a subject we naturally shy away from – a topic that hardly enlivens a party – yet it is one of the certainties of life. Inevitably we will all face death some day. We are mortal beings, and the possibility of death at any moment is with us from the day of our conception.

As babies we depend on our parents to protect us from mortal danger. As young children with the ability to move around and explore the electric socket or the saucepan containing boiling soup, we need protection. As teenagers we are vulnerable to peer pressure and all manner of temptations, for instance, to slide down the self-destructive path of drug abuse.

Throughout our lives carelessness, accidents and illnesses are there lurking, unseen, ready to snare us. It is not just our own carelessness that we have to contend with: someone else's carelessness may impact our lives tragically. Consider the reckless driving of others that kills innocent people on our roads. We may die in wars, terrorist attacks, or natural disasters; or from famine or disease.

We face the possibility of death every day, yet we rarely consider it. We are all, in a sense, on death row! Yet the pleasures and busyness of life blind us to it, unlike those who literally sit on death row awaiting execution. The death of a loved one awakens in us the reality of our own vulnerability. We hear comments such as 'He was not that old – just turned fifty – yet his heart failed him.' Such events alert us, for a brief moment, to the fragility of life. We did not know how bad things were because the deceased sought to shield us, or perhaps he did not wish to dwell on how ill he was.

THE CAUSE OF DEATH

So why do we die? Why do we have to go through this process which often causes so much suffering to us and our loved ones? What is death, and how did it come about? We are born to die. Nobody gets younger; we all age, although many endeavour to mask or deny this.

To answer this fundamental question we need to consider what the Bible says about the subject. Genesis, the first book of the Bible, records the first death. It tells us how the world was created by God and also tells us how God made man. The account in Genesis is hotly disputed by evolutionists. If we want to be god in our lives and usurp the authority of the living God who made us, then like Adam – our direct ancestor – we will not believe the word of God.

We will look at the biblical account in Genesis 2–3 and consider what it says about death. Genesis tells us that God made Adam from the dust of the ground. Then God breathed into his nostrils and gave him life, and so man became a living being (Genesis 2v7).

We read that God took Adam, the first man, and placed him in the Garden of Eden to cultivate it (Genesis 2v15). God told him that he was allowed to eat of every tree in the garden except the tree of the knowledge of good and evil (Genesis 2v16–17). The consequence of disobedience was death. At this time woman did not exist; God had not made her yet.

Then God gave Adam a wife. His wife was created from one of his ribs. The man and his wife were both naked, but not ashamed (Genesis 2v21–25). Then along came the serpent and tricked the woman into eating the forbidden fruit (Genesis 3v1–5). The approach of the serpent is noteworthy. He asks a seemingly harmless question about the restrictions imposed on Adam and Eve. The woman replies that they are only prohibited from eating the fruit of the tree in the middle of the garden, and that if they eat it, or merely touch it, they will die.

God had not commanded the woman directly. Adam was entrusted with the task of passing on this word from God to his wife. So the command had come through Adam, and perhaps he had added the part about not touching it because he did not want her to go near it.

The serpent assures the woman that she will not die. Let us paraphrase the conversation: 'Look, what kind of God do you think he is? He's not going to kill you – destroy the pinnacle of his creation! Believe me, I'm the voice of experience and reason. What God told you is a blatant lie: it's unreasonable, a fairy tale. Where's the evidence? Where's the scientific proof? Do you know of anyone who has died? How many funerals have you been to? Have you buried any pets lately? Of course you haven't. God is lying; he wants to control you – to keep you from making your very own grown-up choices. You need to be broad-minded like me. God doesn't want you to have equality with himself.'

Eve weighs up the argument of the serpent and considers what Adam has said to her. She may have thought, 'How would Adam know God's word? Who does he think he is to boss me around? Adam and I are equal!'

The fruit looks enticing and she desires it. She sees that it is good for food and will make her wise.

There was no evidence of death to help her refute the serpent. God's word received through her husband, and the serpent's preferable alternative which ties in so neatly with her own desire, are in conflict. So she concludes that the cunning serpent appears to be right, and that no harm will come to her. We have not seen God or heaven or hell, just as Eve had no experience of death to call upon. All we have is God's word for it.

She offers some of the fruit to Adam, probably giving him the serpent's assurance. There is no way the man is fooled by the serpent's advice (1 Timothy 2v13–14). That means he deliberately partakes of the fruit. It is probable that he wanted an excuse to try it out, thinking that if God were to complain – and how would he know anyway – he could blame the woman, whom God had made. So it would be God's fault!

Adam ends up deliberately disobeying the command he received from God, his maker. It shows that he did not take God's word seriously. He was full of unbelief.

In effect he was calling God a liar. Sin is unbelief, that is, not believing God's word, and results in disobedience. We may also note that in eating this fruit, Adam and Eve show that they do not believe that God will see what they are doing. When we sin, we sin against God, and we deny that God sees us.

Do we take God's word seriously, and if so, how seriously? Have we opened the Bible today and read from it?

Adam and Eve then realise their error about God not seeing. What happens? They become aware that they are naked and try to cover up by making aprons out of fig leaves. They do this to hide the fact that they have eaten the forbidden fruit, that is, to hide their disobedience, which was a direct result of their unbelief.

Whereas they had previously assumed that eating the forbidden fruit would go unnoticed unless God were to count the fruit, they now realised that their nakedness was further evidence that they needed to hide from God. They came up with 'fig-leaf religion', thinking that when God came walking in the garden, as he often did, they were covered and that he would not notice the new outfit or the missing fruit. By covering themselves with these aprons they think they are covering the fact that they have eaten the forbidden fruit. 'Fig-leaf religion' is the precursor of all man-made religion. It is false. It tries to rectify the problem man's way, and fails. It is not God's way. Only God knows how to resolve the problem. After all, he is the one who has been disobeyed. He, not Adam and Eve, should decide on the solution which will meet his demand for justice. We know that the judgement is already in place for God had told Adam, '... *for in the day that you eat of it you shall die*' *(Genesis 2v17)*.

However, when God comes into the garden they hear him, and they run and hide among the trees. The fig leaves are useless, as is all man-made religion. Adam and Eve did their best to make amends, to hide their sin, but it was not what God wanted. They hid among the trees supposing that it would be dark and that God would not see them. As sinful people, we love darkness rather than light because our deeds are evil. However, God is light, and in him there is no darkness at all (John 3v19–20; 1 John 1v5). Like Adam and Eve, we try to hide our sin and pretend that 'we did not do it' rather than face up to it, own up to God, and look to him for mercy.

We deceive ourselves and others, thinking that our good deeds show that everything is fine – until we come face to face with the living God. We cannot hide from God.

Hebrews 4v13: *And before him no creature is hidden, but all are open and laid bare to the eyes of him with whom we have to do.*

Jeremiah 23v24: *'Can a man hide himself in secret places so that I cannot see him?' says the Lord.*

Disobedience results in fear. Adam tells God that he is afraid because he is naked. He hopes that God will accept his reason and not probe further. But God does probe further: *'Who told you that you were naked? Have you eaten of the tree of which I commanded you not to eat?' (Genesis 3v11).* What line of questioning do we think God will take with us when we stand before him on our own? How will we respond? Will we try to answer like Adam, and blame someone else? However, God questions Adam because he is the head of the family and is therefore responsible. He received the command from God. Eve in turn received it from Adam. Notice too how Adam subtly implicates God: 'You're responsible, God. Don't blame me. You made this woman, so you are ultimately responsible – and if not, she should take the blame. It's not my fault. It's the company I keep, and the tempting environment you've put me in!' (Genesis 3v12, paraphrased).

Genesis 2v17 tells us that the penalty of sin is death. Death means separation. Adam's sin caused an immediate separation from God, that is, a broken relationship (Isaiah 59v2).

The separation of soul and body was deferred. However, while we remain on death row our spirit may be brought to life. This is called 'rebirth' or 'being born again'. Just as God's breath gave Adam life, so the Holy Spirit gives eternal life to those who believe (John 3v7).

If you haven't been born again you could ask God to give you this new birth now, as you read this book.

Genesis 3v19 tells us that we are to expect the death of our bodies: ... *you are dust, and to dust you shall return.* When our bodies die there is no more opportunity for new birth. All of us will be restored to life after we die physically, and we will be given new bodies. The restoration to life of the spirit can only take place during our life on earth. The Bible, referring to physical life, tells us that we die once, and then comes judgement. After this there is no further physical death. This is only good news for those who have been born again. The rest will stand condemned before the judgement throne of God, and will be *thrown into the lake of fire (Revelation 20).* God's desire is for us to avoid eternal damnation and receive eternal life. This is why he has given us a warning (2 Peter 3v9).

Spiritual death means a broken relationship with God. We die because we are descended from Adam. We were in

Adam when he sinned. In 1 Corinthians 15v22 we read, *For as in Adam all die, so also in Christ shall all be made alive.* This means that to be delivered from eternal damnation we need to be 'in Christ'.

This concept of being 'in Adam' is paralleled in Hebrews 7v9–10, which says of Levi the priest: *One might even say that Levi himself, who receives tithes, paid tithes through Abraham, for he was still in the loins of his ancestor when Melchiz'edek met him.* The writer to the Hebrews is saying that when Abraham paid tithes to Melchizedek, Levi was present in Abraham and paying tithes too. Levi was a great-grandson of Abraham, and was not even born when Abraham paid tithes to Melchizedek. In fact Abraham was childless at this point.

However, this is very useful for us because it helps us to see that we were present in Adam when he sinned in the garden. It is his sin that is the problem. We sin now, that is, we show the symptoms of our sinful nature because we have inherited Adam's nature. The only way we could not be sinners is if we were not descended from Adam. Therefore, if we can show that we are not descended from Adam, then:

- we are not under condemnation;
- we are not accountable;
- we have not sinned; and
- we should not die.

Then why do we fear death? And why will we die?

We deduced earlier that when our ancestor Adam sinned we were 'present', though obviously not yet born. We were 'in his loins'.

We see in Adam's disobedience the classic case of caving into temptation on the grounds of diminished responsibility, and hiding behind the 'authority' of another (James 1v13–15).

After they had disobeyed God, Adam and Eve had been content, happy that this problem had been resolved, until God turned up. When God came looking they hid from his presence. This is amazing; so much for the fig-leaf solution. It was blown apart by God's presence. They were afraid, and they hid further in the darkness of the trees. They knew that they were naked and that they were guilty. This awareness pointed to their disobedience. Their aprons and their attempts to hide among the trees failed. We can hide our sin from one another and from ourselves, but our misdeeds will be exposed by God. We cannot hide our sin from him.

When God probes Adam he acknowledges the sin, but not his responsibility for it. How lucky we are when God comes searching and asks 'Where are you?' He does so because he desires our repentance. He loves us. Those who trust in their good deeds will try to flee from God in fear that their deeds will be exposed for what they are.

God made garments from animal skins for Adam and Eve. This meant that blood was shed. A sacrifice was made. This sacrifice pointed to God's true solution for our sin – the cross of Christ. John the Baptist said of Jesus, *'Behold, the Lamb of God, who takes away the sin of the world!'* (*John 1v29).*

Fig-leaf religion was also exposed by Jesus (Mark 11v12–20). The fig tree was full of leaves but bore no fruit. It was a charade; a pretence; it was all show and utterly useless! It was like the religious practice of the Pharisees. Mark interrupts the account of the fig tree being cursed with his narrative of the cleansing of the temple by Jesus. The religious rulers were enraged by Jesus. They sought the praise of men and obtained it with showy religious razzmatazz, but they were fruitless and powerless. They did not produce the fruit of a godly life. They were devoid of the Spirit of God. Jesus sought the fruit of godliness in them – and why not – for the Son of God was entitled to demand this.

Let us move on and consider another question. Who was the first person to die? Was it Abel, who was murdered by his brother Cain? (Genesis 4; 1 John 3v11–12).

Certainly, Abel's death equates to what we commonly mean by death, where a person's body and soul part company. In this sense Abel was the first to die. Had he not been murdered by Cain he would have eventually died. We need to understand, however, that this was not the earliest death. Adam's death happened the moment he ate the forbidden fruit. Something happened to him that day. He became spiritually dead to God. His physical death happened many years later. In effect, he needed to be reborn. When he died spiritually, we all died, and we all need rebirth. Nicodemus, referred to in John 3, did us a great favour. This intellectual teacher of the law asked Jesus important questions about rebirth.

WHAT DO WE MEAN BY DEATH?

There are some who believe that there is nothing beyond death, while others believe that they will be reincarnated.

Firstly, we need to consider briefly the term 'death' because the Bible tells us that there is a second death (Revelation 20), which would indicate that there is a first death. When we speak of death we usually refer to physical death, and this is, in effect, the first death. This death is a process characterised by ageing, and it has an end point.

We have already stated that people die once, according to Hebrews 9v27. This verse is speaking of physical death.

So how are we to understand 'the second death'? If we have died, then to die a second time we must first be restored to life. Indeed, we will all stand before God in new physical bodies and he will judge us. It would be natural to view the second death through the filter of our understanding of the first death. This may lead to an incorrect assumption that the second death is an end point like physical death. So, we may wrongly conclude that after the second death we will just cease to exist, i.e. life would come to an end, like our physical life on earth ends. In fact the second death is continuous. It does not have an end point. We are told very plainly in Revelation 20 that the second death is 'the lake of fire'. We commonly refer to it as hell. It is where the Devil, that is, Satan, and his team will be thrown. Day and night they will be tormented for ever and ever (Revelation 20v10). There is no relief for anyone who ends up there! The words 'for ever and ever' point to the second death being continuous.

Having introduced the term judgement, we now need to consider this, in particular, its certainty.

THE CERTAINTY OF JUDGEMENT

> ... *it is appointed for men to die once, and after that comes judgment (Hebrews 9v27).*

There are some who would argue that when we die we go to a place they call 'purgatory' where we are given a second chance to redeem ourselves, and that when we become good enough, we enter heaven. However, the Bible clearly tells us that after death we face judgement. We are not given a second chance.

As mentioned earlier, there are those who say that we will be reincarnated – that we will come back, for example, as a different person – depending on what we have done in this life. However, the Bible says that we die once and after that we are judged.

There are those who teach, wrongly, that there is no second death – that those who are condemned merely cease to exist. This belief is called annihilationism. It is a false teaching. After we die physically we will be given new bodies and stand before God. These new bodies will never die physically. Physical death is a one-off event. Then God will pass judgement and those whose names are written in the Book of Life will not be cast into the lake of fire.

However, those whose names are not written in the Book of Life will be cast into the lake of fire. They will not die physically (Revelation 20v14–15). This lake of fire is a place of everlasting torment, day and night, without relief. It is a place to be avoided.

Perhaps we have been told about the lake of fire and how to avoid it, and yet in our pride and folly we have ignored the warnings. You are reading this today, so it is not too late for you. You do not have to go there.

Physical death is a mercy from God because it focuses the mind on our predicament – that all of us will face judgement one day – and warns us of our need of a saviour. We are told of our need to put our trust in God's word.

'What folly,' we say! 'Take away this place called hell. What God of love lets anyone go to hell?'

Adam's physical death sentence started the moment he disobeyed God and ate the forbidden fruit. His relationship with God was broken. However, God in his mercy gave Adam a window of opportunity to be restored to fellowship with himself. We too have such an opportunity to be reconciled with God. Those who do so will escape the second death which is the lake of fire (Revelation 20v14–15).

If the thief on the cross got his name written in the Book of Life then it must be pretty simple. When Jesus was crucified, two thieves were crucified on either side of him. One of them asked Jesus to remember him when he came into his kingdom. Jesus told him that he would be in paradise with him that day (Luke 23v39–43).

HOW DO WE GET OUR NAMES ENTERED IN THE BOOK OF LIFE?

- We need to acknowledge to God that we are sinners and deserve eternal punishment;
- We need to believe the message of the gospel that Jesus Christ, God's only Son, became a man so that he might die on a cross to pay the penalty for all of our sins;
- We need to trust that the death of Jesus Christ on the cross is sufficient to pay the penalty for our sins.

God's provision is the way of escape, the only way of escape, for us. We are to look to Jesus Christ on the cross. His death on the cross paid the penalty for our sin. All we need to do is ask for the free pardon God offers us, because Jesus took the punishment for us.

- It requires faith;
- It requires that we honour God by trusting his promise;
- The second death is eternal torment – there is no physical death to escape it;
- The only way to escape the second death is to look to Jesus.

We have seen that judgement follows death. We will now turn our attention to how we might be judged.

17

Chapter Three

How Will We Be Judged?

... it is appointed for men to die once, and after that comes judgment (Hebrews 9v27).

From this quotation we learn that physical death comes to all of us once, and that judgement follows death.

We are being told plainly that there is no second chance; this life is it. We will not be reincarnated. We do not get the chance to make amends in another life, or in 'purgatory'. There is no such place. Our window of opportunity to be reconciled to God is limited to one lifespan, and it is indeed a blessed mercy of God that we have even this. Why is this so? When Adam sinned God could have killed him there and then but, in his mercy, God gave him the opportunity to repent. We are the way we are because we are descended from this one man, Adam, and have inherited his sinful nature. Our sinful nature manifests itself outwardly in our actions and speech, and inwardly in our thinking.

The concept of judgement is one with which we should all be familiar. It occurs in our lives in some form every day. We rely on this concept to live. Judgement is comparison; it is measurement. We judge distances. We use weights and measures when we buy and sell fruit, vegetables, milk, beer, curtains, carpets and petrol, relying on accurate balances or meters. A man may be measured up for a suit or a coffin.

For measurement to be just, we need to have recognised standards, set and agreed. Hence we have miles, pounds, pints, and their metric equivalents. There must be consistency and integrity.

Employees undergo performance appraisals where their performance is measured against previously agreed targets. Students have their performance measured by sitting examinations. The general population has its health checked by comparison with a set of standards that is considered to be the norm.

So how do we measure our performance, and how would we give account of our lives to God our maker? By what standards will we be judged?

Our natural tendency is to compare ourselves with others, perhaps because we got used to checking our academic performance with our peer group during our school days. When we compare ourselves with others we make ourselves the standard by which we measure them. We may feel happy with this because, although we are not the top performer, we can at least point to someone worse than us. We have a built-in bias to excuse those 'understandable' and 'minor' blemishes that we ourselves have. Sometimes we are just blind to our own faults.

Perhaps we should consider a more objective standard, for example, the Ten Commandments. This might be a useful gauge against which we could measure ourselves. How do we fare against this yardstick?

THE TEN COMMANDMENTS

The Ten Commandments were given by God to the people of Israel after he had redeemed the Israelites from slavery in Egypt. God was to be their God and they were to be his people. It was a covenant between God and Israel that required the Israelites to live in accordance with God's ways. The Ten Commandments are set out in Exodus 20v1–17.

In Mark 10v17–22 a man asks Jesus what he must do to inherit eternal life. Jesus lists some of the Ten Commandments:

- Do not kill;
- Do not commit adultery;
- Do not steal;
- Do not bear false witness;
- Do not defraud;
- Honour your father and mother.

The man responds by telling Jesus that he has kept all of these since he was a youth, but he knows in his heart that this is not enough.

The commandments that Jesus listed relate to loving people. Jesus did not list the other commandments, that relate to loving God. He then introduces the commandments in the latter category, homing in on covetousness, that is, idolatry. The man's wealth was his idol – his god. Jesus tells him plainly: follow me, not your riches; make me your God; trust me – not your wealth.

We will consider the Ten Commandments and show how breaking them can be regarded as theft. They are listed in the table which follows the definition of the term theft.

WHAT IS THEFT?

The most obvious form of theft is unlawfully taking goods that belong to another. It can also be defined as depriving someone of their rightful due, either deliberately or negligently. It is to withhold from someone that which rightly belongs to them, or to cause it to be withheld by not taking requisite action. It could be giving to someone the credit due to another. It could be failure to pay a debt, or it could be damage caused to the property or reputation of another.

When did we last give to God the praise and thanksgiving due to him?

God's Commandments in brief	
You shall:	Stealing/Theft
– have no other gods before me.	To steal God's glory in creation and redemption by attributing it to someone, or something else, e.g. the golden calf (Exodus 32).
– not worship idols.	To steal God's glory in creation and redemption.

– not take God's name in vain.	Theft of reputation – blaming God, attributing to God evil motives, e.g. God was said to have taken the Israelites out of Egypt because there was no room in Egypt to bury them there.
	Theft of authority – pretending to have his authority, e.g. false prophets claiming to speak for God.
– keep the Sabbath day holy.	To deprive yourself and others of rest.
	To deprive God of a day set apart for him.
– honour your father and mother.	To withhold provision from your parents in their old age (Mark 7), e.g. welfare, courtesy and burial.
	To besmirch their reputation.
– not kill.	To steal someone's life.

(continued)

God's Commandments in brief	
You shall:	**Stealing/Theft**
– not commit adultery.	To steal another's spouse. Theft or destruction of one or more relationships.
– not steal.	To steal another's possessions, ideas, or rights.
– not bear false witness.	To steal another's reputation.
– not covet.	To steal God's glory is idolatry. *... Coveting, which is idolatry (Ephesians 5v5).*

Coveting is illicitly desiring something that rightly belongs to another, or seeking to deprive them of it. Greed or hatred will often be the motive behind this.

Have we ever withheld from God the praise that is rightly due to him and him alone?

Have we ever attributed to God's creation the glory that is in fact due to God, thus depriving him of worship?

When we consider the commandments honestly we will conclude that we do not meet the required standard, for the standard we must achieve is perfection.

> *For whoever keeps the whole law but fails in one point has become guilty of all of it (James 2v10).*

WHO IS THE JUDGE?

We considered earlier how we tend to judge ourselves by comparison with others. There is one problem with that:

We will not be the judge; this will not be self-appraisal. We will be judged by Jesus Christ (John 5v22–23; Acts 17v30–31), and he will judge us by comparison with himself (Romans 2v16). Our yardstick is Jesus. Jesus Christ was sinless. Which of us would claim to be sinless? (Romans 3v23; Ecclesiastes 7v20).

THE CONSEQUENCE OF JUDGEMENT

When we are measured against Jesus Christ we will be shown to fall short of his standard – by a long way. This means that God's wrath rests upon us and he ought to send us to hell. Hell is the place of eternal torment.

How serious is this threat?

How bad is this place called hell?

The threat is very serious, and the place is unimaginably bad. This is why God sent his only Son to this earth to suffer a horrendous death on a cross so that God's wrath might be appeased, and our sins paid for. Be sure of this: God's wrath will not be turned aside for those who spurn his Son (Hebrews 10v28-29).

How shall we escape this terrible, everlasting punishment?

How might we be saved or delivered?

There is a way of escape, and we shall consider this when we consider Jesus Christ in chapters 8 and 9. Next, however, we will consider the Ten Commandments in more detail.

Chapter Four

The Ten Commandments: How Do I Measure up?

BACKGROUND

The people of Israel had been enslaved in Egypt for about four hundred years. They cried out to God about their plight, and God responded. Their captivity had been foretold to Abraham (Genesis 15). God sent Moses to lead the Israelites out of Egypt. The details of this part of Israel's history may be found in Exodus 3–20. Through his servant Moses God performed signs and wonders, the last of which was to kill all the firstborn of both man and beast. Note that the term 'firstborn' does not necessarily refer just to the young; the firstborn could have been of any age. The term relates to the order of birth. This may be stating the obvious, but it is easy to overlook the point. This was a devastating judgement on the people of Egypt. The Israelites were told to partake in a Passover meal that night, and to apply the blood of a lamb to the doorposts of their homes (Exodus 12v13). This was an act of faith in obedience to what seemed a strange command from God. It was also a matter of life and death. Applying this blood would cause the angel of death to pass over their homes without harming the firstborn. They were also required to eat the flesh of this Passover lamb.

The Egyptians responded to this tragedy by expelling the Israelites from their land, and so the Israelites came to Mount Sinai where God gave them the Ten Commandments. They had taken three months to reach Mount Sinai (Exodus 19v1). It was not long then, after the exodus, that despite all the signs and wonders that God had performed through Moses, and the judgement that God had executed on Egypt's gods, Israel turned to idolatry. The time gap would have been about four months.

The Lord had taken Israel to be his people and he was to be their God. In the light of this, we come to the first commandment.

THE FIRST COMMANDMENT

I am the LORD your God, who brought you out of the land of Egypt, out of the house of bondage. You shall have no other gods before me (Exodus 20v2–3).

The first commandment reminds Israel of their redemption from slavery, and demands that credit for this deliverance be given to the Lord alone and no one else.

We are told that the Israelites had arrived at Sinai on the third new moon and that Moses was on Mount Sinai for forty days with God (Exodus 19v1, 24v18). In Exodus 32v1–6 we have an account of what they did while Moses was away. They gave up on Moses and made a golden calf to replace

God, and worshipped it, giving it credit for rescuing them from slavery in Egypt, even though it did not exist in Egypt. Note how absurd this was: they made a lifeless image after they had been away from Egypt for just about four months. This was worship that was rightfully due to God alone, and giving it to an idol deprived God of what was his. It was theft. They had robbed God.

Salvation belongs to God alone; he has done this for you and me. He has redeemed us from the curse of the law (Galatians 3v13). By rejecting Christ we rob him of the glory due to him alone and give it either to ourselves by trusting in our own good works to save us, or to some religious leader or religion.

> *He who does not honour the Son does not honour the Father who sent him (John 5v23).*

The first commandment deals with the glory due to God alone for his acts of redemption from slavery, the first of which was a prophetic precursor for the second. The Passover lamb in Egypt pointed to the true Passover Lamb, Jesus Christ, of whom John the Baptist said: *'Behold, the Lamb of God ...'* (John 1v29).

THE SECOND COMMANDMENT

> *You shall not make for yourself a graven image, or any likeness of anything that is in heaven above, or that is in the earth beneath, or that is in the water under the earth; you shall not bow down to them or serve them; for I the Lord your God am a jealous God, visiting the iniquity of the fathers upon the children to the third and fourth generation of those who hate me, but showing steadfast*

love to thousands of those who love me and keep my commandments (Exodus 20v4–6).

The second commandment is concerned with creation. Here, we are forbidden to make and worship idols representing any part of creation. Giving glory to an inanimate object, worshipping some aspect of creation, or perhaps attributing glory to 'mother nature' or science, detracts from God. It robs him of worship (Romans 1v20–23). It could be giving glory to a human idea. Science is, of course, man's knowledge, and so, man is effectively worshipping man when he praises science. The theory of evolution is one such attempt to rob God of credit due to him so that we do not have to submit to his rule.

God will not share his glory with other gods (Isaiah 42v8).

THE THIRD COMMANDMENT

You shall not take the name of the Lord your God in vain; for the Lord will not hold him guiltless who takes his name in vain (Exodus 20v7).

This commandment refers to the wrongful use of the name of God. When someone says 'Christ!' he is attributing blame to Jesus Christ. He is diminishing Christ's glory – tarnishing Christ's reputation. He is robbing Christ.

However, this command is addressed to God's people in the first instance. How then does the Christian take God's name in vain?

The name of Christ is attached to the Christian, so when a Christian misbehaves he tarnishes Christ's reputation. This provides the non-Christian with the excuse to say, 'I will not go to church because it is full of hypocrites.'

The Christian may sometimes use Christ's name or God's name to strengthen his position with, or intimidate, other Christians. 'God told me...' These words put a stop to discourse, the implication being that anything you question or dispute is wrong since you are questioning God. This malpractice has serious consequences.

> ... the Lord will not hold him guiltless who takes his name in vain (Exodus 20v7).

When the Christian uses the name of Christ to give weight to his own word he is stealing authority from Christ. He has no right to use the name of Christ in this way. It is like a forged signature. It is using Christ's name dishonestly. Furthermore, it is quite a common practice among people to use the name of Jesus thus: 'What would Jesus say?' Sometimes they want to think about what Jesus would say in certain situations, and their question is sincere. However, people often use this question as a means of stifling argument or discourse. They claim the moral high ground and imply that they speak on behalf of Jesus – that they know that he would approve their words and deeds. They claim to speak for the one whom they damn with their faint praise and reject with their lifestyle. Judas Iscariot was one of their number. See how he purported to speak for Jesus (John 12v3–6). Mary, the sister of Lazarus whom Jesus had restored to life from the dead, anointed the feet of Jesus with some very expensive ointment which she poured out. The words that fell from the mouth of Judas were, *'Why was this ointment not sold for three hundred denarii and given to the poor?'* (John 12 v5).

So, people often raise the question, 'What would Jesus say?' not because they want to know the answer, but rather because they think they have the answer and want to seize the moral high ground. This is the Jesus of their imagination, not the historical figure recorded in the Bible. They usually misinterpret Jesus, either wilfully or through ignorance. They play the same game as the man who says, 'God told me.' It is taking the name of the Lord in vain.

We will surely know the answer to the question 'What would Jesus say?' when we stand before Jesus. All of us will stand before him and find out what he has to say.

THE FOURTH COMMANDMENT

> *Remember the Sabbath day, to keep it holy. Six days you shall labour, and do all your work; but the seventh day is a Sabbath to the Lord your God; in it you shall not do any work, you, or your son, or your daughter, your manservant, or your maidservant, or your cattle, or the sojourner who is within your gates; for in six days the Lord made heaven and earth, the sea and all that is in them, and rested the seventh day; therefore the Lord blessed the Sabbath day and hallowed it (Exodus 20v8–11).*

The Sabbath, that is the seventh day of the week, was given to Israel for the benefit of the people of God as:

- a day to rest from their labours;
- a day to reflect on the week and give thanks to God;
- a day to pray for the week ahead;
- a day for fellowship with God's people;
- a day for corporate worship not enjoyed during the six busy working days;
- a day set apart for a people set apart.

It was also to be a sign of distinction of God's people. *'Moreover I gave them my Sabbaths, as a sign between me and them, that they might know that I the Lord sanctify them' (Ezekiel 20v12).*

'... and hallow my Sabbaths that they may be a sign between me and you, that you may know that I the LORD am your God' (Ezekiel 20v20).

To 'hallow the Sabbath day' means to set it apart as distinct from other days – to make it special rather than ordinary. It is not 'business as usual' – not seeking private goals.

Keeping the Sabbath day requires careful forethought: for example, in Exodus 16, the people of Israel were commanded to gather a double portion of manna on the sixth day and not to gather on the seventh day. On the other hand, the concept of Sabbath day rest refers to the ordinary course of life, and not to emergencies. *'The Sabbath was made for man, not man for the Sabbath ...' (Mark 2v27).*

It was a Sabbath to the Lord, the God of Israel. Those in Israel who were not to work on the Sabbath were listed in Exodus 20v8–11 as:

- you;
- your son and daughter;
- your man servant and maid servant;
- your cattle;
- your lodger ('sojourner').

The list thus covered the Israelites and all who took shelter under them, their authority and their protection, that is, those for whom they were responsible.

The Sabbath was God's design for man and his labours. God himself set the pattern by deliberately ordering his creation in six days. The task was started and finished in six days as planned. God is a God of order. One step follows another; he is the master of critical path analysis. Foundations are followed by superstructures. The Sabbath day is special to God and it was he who set it apart from the other days. He has shown his children how to work:

- in an orderly manner;
- in a planned manner;
- with each step accomplished within its allotted time frame.

If God had not created the world in six days and rested on the seventh, then there would be no need to rest on the Sabbath.

The Sabbath day rest affirms God's six-day creation.

Keeping the Sabbath demonstrates faith in the six-day creation. Failure to keep it also deprives us, and those for whom we are responsible, of rest.

THE FIFTH COMMANDMENT

> *Honour your father and your mother, that your days may be long in the land which the LORD your God gives you (Exodus 20v12).*

Our parents bring us into the world and are responsible for nurturing and teaching us. To honour our parents means to submit to or to obey them. It does not mean we should not question their judgement, but that we should submit to their decisions nevertheless; it means that we are to accept their authority over us. As we grow older the balance of the relationship will shift as we take on more responsibility for ourselves. Later on we will have responsibility for looking after them in their old age. In our society this responsibility has been usurped, to a large extent, by the state.

We should respect our parents' opinions and seek their advice (they know us very well and should give us objective advice on our decision-making). We should give them our time – our precious time.

Do nothing that will bring them shame. Live in an honourable way so that the family name is not brought into disrepute in the community. Obviously there are exceptions to this, for following Jesus can bring perceived shame to a family. In some places where there is a strong religious culture, difficulties arise for the family of the one who becomes a Christian. Obedience to Christ overrides this.

The examples of honouring parents that I include here are, in fact, those of two people who honoured their in-laws.

Moses honoured his wife's father who had 'adopted' him (Exodus 18v7). He showed respect to Jethro when they met, with his deference. He spent time with his father-in-law. Exodus 18v19, 24 tells us that Moses listened to his father-in-law and took his advice. This is the great Moses, appointed by God to lead Israel out of Egypt, showing great humility and wisdom in listening to his father-in-law and taking his advice. We may note too that this is the Moses who brought shame to his foster mother, the daughter of Pharaoh, by rejecting the wealth and prestige of Egypt in order to follow Jesus Christ (Hebrews 11v24–26).

Providing for parents means not being selfish or self-centred. It means having respect for your spouse's parents too. It means not hiding wicked, selfish desires behind the facade of religion (Mark 7v6–13).

Ruth was someone who honoured her mother-in-law (Ruth 1v16–17). *'All that you have done for your mother-in-law since the death of your husband has been fully told me ...,'* says

Boaz (Ruth 2v11). Ruth had left home to look after a widow who was bereft of her two sons and had no means of support. It is not surprising that Boaz should admire these qualities in Ruth, for he was like-minded.

We honour our parents in death when we bury them. We can honour or dishonour them post-death through our memory and how we speak of them, that is:

- with love or hatred;
- with warmth or coolness;
- with pride or shame.

However, we must not worship or idolise our parents, as we have noted in considering the first two commandments. Ancestor-worship is wrong.

THE SIXTH COMMANDMENT

You shall not kill (Exodus 20v13).

This command of the Lord is increasingly ignored. There has been much reporting of 'knife crime' among the young, and it often results in death.

Now, Jesus says hatred too is murder, for Jesus looks at the heart.

- Why is there so much killing?
- Why is life undervalued?
- Why is there a decline in self-control?

Do you ever wonder why someone could have no qualms about murder, and even do it 'for kicks'? The answer is because for several generations we have increasingly turned our backs on God, and in our pride, have believed that we are getting better – that we are evolving into a better race. We no longer fear God and, indeed, many deny his existence. We do not acknowledge him, and say that science is all that matters.

There is no fear of God before their eyes (Romans 3v18).

In Britain this is a major problem which the church, the body of God's people, has yet to take seriously. We spend much time 'rearranging the flowers', while many are preparing to 'push up the daisies'.

What should we do?

- Indulge ourselves with our creature comforts?
- Retreat into our man-made fortresses?
- Bury our heads in the sand?

No!

The solution is not politics or economics.

The starting point is to turn to Almighty God in prayer (2 Chronicles 20v12).

We see the nation enslaved and disintegrating before our very eyes.

'For how can I endure to see the calamity that is coming to my people? Or how can I endure to see the destruction of my kindred?' (Esther 8v6).

THE SEVENTH COMMANDMENT

You shall not commit adultery (Exodus 20v14).

37

Adultery is forbidden. Why is this so? It shows the importance of marriage and how God views marriage. Just as it is only God who converts people, so we learn that God alone joins a man and a woman together in marriage. *What therefore God has joined together, let not man put asunder (Mark 10v9).*

Marriage is a relationship based on a promise between a man and a woman in the sight of God and witnesses. For a man and woman to live together in a relationship without the exchange of vows, that is, without a commitment being made in public, is folly. There can never be an assurance that either party will not walk away; there is nothing binding. The same is true for a marriage with a prenuptial agreement. Each party will know what is *his* and what is *hers* rather than what is *theirs*. It is true that many marriages do end in divorce, but it is harder for married couples to separate.

Would we like a relationship with God where he could walk away at any time? If this were the case then we could never have confidence in God. Our lives as Christians, should we become Christians, would be paralysed by fear, and our faith, trust and confidence in God would never grow. Faith grows as we get to know God and understand what he wants, as we experience his answers to our prayers and as we learn about him through studying his Word, the Bible.

Often God likens idolatry, that is, breaking a covenant relationship with God, to adultery. Marriage mirrors God's relationship with his people. *For this reason a man shall leave his father and mother and be joined to his wife, and the two shall become one flesh. This mystery is a profound one, and I am saying that it refers to Christ and the church (Ephesians 5v31–32).*

Note also God's Word for our guidance in the book of Proverbs to preserve us from the 'adventuress' with her 'smooth tongue' (Proverbs 6v23–35). The adulteress is a danger to man for she stalks his life, and a jealous husband cannot be compensated. Proverbs compares the sin of going to a prostitute with that of adultery. Both are wrong, but the consequences of the latter are more damaging because there is a relationship that is formed.

Jesus tackled two sides of this sin: divorce (Mark 10v 2–12) and lust (Matthew 5v27–28).

Whoever divorces his wife and marries another, commits adultery against her ... (Mark 10v11).

Matthew 5v27–29 tells us that the problem is not simply about the physical act of adultery. Jesus says that if we look at a woman lustfully we have already committed adultery with her in our hearts. We must take radical steps to avoid it, going so far as to pluck out the offending eye and throw it away. However, literally plucking out an eye is not what is meant here, for this will not prevent lustful thoughts, which begin in our hearts. It does, however, show the seriousness of this sin and that is why such a drastic remedy is suggested.

In the book of Judges 13–16 we have an account of Samson, who was a very strong man. His strength was dependent on him never cutting his hair. He had a weakness for beautiful women, one of whom teased the secret of his strength from him. She then had her people, the Philistines, cut his hair and imprison him. The irony of Samson's weakness was that his eyes were literally plucked out by the Philistines because of his sin and this led to his weakness no longer being fed, and all he could 'focus' on was God's work, that is, God's purpose for him. This is a sobering thought to guide all of us!

What is it that keeps us from fulfilling God's purpose for our lives?

What distractions do we have?

What private schemes of self-fulfilment, pleasure, fame or fortune get in the way which God may yet deal with?

God used Samson's enemies to destroy his weakness.

Joseph's secret in resisting Potiphar's wife is found in Genesis 39v10: *And although she spoke to Joseph day after day, he would not listen to her, to lie with her or to be with her.* He did not contemplate this opportunity; he avoided it because he feared God.

THE EIGHTH COMMANDMENT

You shall not steal (Exodus 20v15).

Steal is an all-embracing word. What kinds of stealing are there?

Theft of goods is the obvious one. Stealing is taking something that does not belong to you. It is depriving someone of their property or rights, like the shoplifter who exits the supermarket without paying for goods or the person who illegally copies a DVD rather than buying an original.

Then there is the theft of ideas, music and software, which deprives the owner of royalties and fame. Corporations infringe patent rights and end up being sued by the owner of the rights.

Theft is also robbing God when worship is not whole-hearted or when giving to God is done grudgingly (Malachi 1v14, 3v8).

There is also the theft of praise. God is rightly due praise, for he is our creator. He made our beautiful world and the wonderful creatures in it, including the cream of the crop, man and woman.

Psalm 111v2 says, *Great are the works of the LORD, studied by all who have pleasure in them,* whilst Romans 1v21 tells us … *for although they knew God they did not honour him as God or give thanks to him …*

Theft can be the giving of what is due to God to someone or something else. When someone else gets credit for something we have done, it naturally riles us. Now, think how God must have felt when the Israelites made a golden calf and attributed honour to it for having rescued them from slavery in Egypt.

> … *and they said 'These are your gods, O Israel, who brought you up out of the land of Egypt!' (Exodus 32v4).*

A further example of theft is the withholding of something rightly due to another on the pretext of religion. Jews were allowed to withhold money from ageing parents by pledging it to the priests. Thus they would shirk their responsibility of honouring their parents (Mark 7v9–13).

Not giving our hearts to Jesus is another form of theft. We can do this when we praise God with our worship songs while neutering his Word, or watering it down to fit in with our lifestyle. We dishonour him by our disobedience. *'Why do you call me "Lord, Lord," and not do what I tell you?' (Luke 6v46).*

When David bought the threshing floor so that he might stop a plague, the owner had wanted to give it to David free of charge. *But King David said to Ornan, 'No, but I will buy it for the full price; I will not take for the LORD what is yours, nor offer burnt offerings which cost me nothing.' (1 Chronicles 21v24).*

It may be that David remembered Nathan's parable (2 Samuel 12v1–7) regarding Uriah and Bathsheba. Nathan had told David of a rich man who had many sheep. He needed to feed a guest, but instead of taking a lamb from his own flock and roasting it, he stole a poor man's only lamb and served it to his guest. This parable was told by Nathan as a device for convicting David of his sin. On hearing it, David was angered by the injustice. Then Nathan applied the parable to David, saying: 'You are the man.'

What had David done? We are told of David's sin in the account leading up to this story. It shows two aspects of theft:

- Theft of a man's wife: Bathsheba was the wife of Uriah the Hittite, and David had slept with her.
- Theft of a man's life: David murdered Uriah when Bathsheba found herself pregnant by David.

In a manner of speaking, before he lost his life, Uriah had virtually lost it already through betrayal. He had been filled with a passion to serve his king and had risked his life in service for his God, his king and his country. He had been willing to die for his king. He loved Bathsheba, his adulterous wife who betrayed him. To have lived with the betrayal by his wife and his king would have been a slow, consuming death.

We can also rob God of our time with self-seeking agendas of pleasure, wealth, and fame.

THE NINTH COMMANDMENT

You shall not bear false witness against your neighbour (Exodus 20v16).

What is false witness?

Why is it done?

In a film called *Atonement* a young girl with a highly imaginative mind has categorised a man as a sex maniac. Later in the film, following a rape, she is convinced, from her prejudgement of him, that he is guilty, and she actually testifies that this innocent party is guilty. The consequences of this are horrific for him and his girlfriend. This is, of course, a fictional account, but it nevertheless demonstrates a motive for false testimony and how it could arise. The girl was blinded by prejudice.

So what is false testimony? It means fabricating an account about someone, usually with an intent to harm them. Perhaps the motive is to make the accused look bad in the eyes of others. Perhaps it is to have the accused put out of the way, as with another fictional case, that of Edmond Dantès in *The Count of Monte Cristo* by Alexander Dumas.

False testimony means lying about someone's character or deeds. It may be motivated by hatred or jealousy. There are several biblical accounts of false testimonies.

Yet, in spite of the suffering of the victim, we learn that God is in control and working out his purpose in spite of the evil deeds of men and women through the ages.

Potiphar's wife lied about Joseph's righteous behaviour when he refused to sleep with her. She accused him of attempted rape. He had refused her attempts to seduce him because he feared the living God. She felt rejected, insulted and humiliated by this Hebrew slave who turned her down and disobeyed her order (Genesis 39v12).

The most wicked lies ever told were about Jesus Christ, God's only Son. These lies were told by the religious leaders in Israel. They were jealous of him. He was a threat to their way of life, their peaceful coexistence with the Romans, and their very livelihood (John 11v48–52).

They were also jealous of his popularity, power, success and authority. Matthew 27v18 says of Pilate: *For he knew that it was out of envy that they had delivered him up.*

They accused him of casting out demons by Beelzebub, the prince of demons. This, in fact, amounted to the blasphemy of the Holy Spirit (Mark 3v28–30). It is the only sin which cannot be pardoned. It is the only sin that can keep us out of heaven. It is the rejection of the Holy Spirit, or the refusal to believe the testimony of the Holy Spirit about the person of Jesus Christ, namely who he is and what he has done. The Holy Spirit glorifies and reveals Jesus Christ to us. To reject this is to reject the only way that we can be saved from hell and go to heaven. It is that important.

> *Now the chief priests and the whole council sought false testimony against Jesus that they might put him to death, but they found none, though many false witnesses came forward (Matthew 26v59–60).*

The express purpose of the religious authorities was to murder Jesus – an emotive word, but nonetheless true. They could not simply stab him because of their hypocrisy for, to them, that would have been murder and might also have led to a riot. So they looked for an excuse to officially put him to death, under the law. They brought in false witnesses to testify against him. They would have been paid handsomely, and yet these witnesses could not agree with one another.

Finally they provoked a response from the key witness, Jesus himself, and they dismissed all the false witnesses. How did they provoke a response from Jesus, who until then had not been answering their charges? The only way they could find grounds for complaint against him was in connection with the law of his God (Daniel 6v5).

The law at issue was the one that stated that when someone was put on oath to testify, he must not remain silent (Leviticus 5v1). The religious leaders were not aware of this, and thus the result of the high priest's demand for Jesus to testify surprised them. The high priest, in a fit of anger, publicly commanded Jesus to testify.

> *'I adjure you by the living God, tell us if you are the Christ ...' (Matthew 26v63).*

If Jesus had remained silent, and refused to testify under oath the truth about his identity, this would have been sin.

Jesus testified publicly under solemn oath that he was the Son of God. In their prejudice they accused him of blasphemy (John 19v7). It is not surprising that in the early years of the church, one of the followers of Jesus got similar treatment. Stephen was lied against and put to death. Here was a man who, we are told, was full of the Holy Spirit (Acts 7v55). They hated him and his testimony.

In his defence against the false accusations directed at him, Stephen gets to the heart of the matter, saying: *'You stiff-necked people, uncircumcised in heart and ears, you always resist the Holy Spirit. As your fathers did, so do you. Which of the prophets did not your fathers persecute?' (Acts 7v51–52).*

Note how Stephen says, '*you always resist the Holy Spirit*'. This is not blasphemy of the Holy Spirit. Saul of Tarsus was there and was one of those resisting the Holy Spirit: '*Saul, Saul, why do you persecute me? It hurts you to kick against the goads' (Acts 26v14)*. Saul was resisting what he was coming to realise was the truth about Jesus of Nazareth, because it did not fit with his own ideas and theological understanding. He was resisting, but not rejecting, the Holy Spirit. If resisting the Holy Spirit were the blasphemy of the Holy Spirit, the only unpardonable sin, then none of us could ever be pardoned. We have all resisted the Holy Spirit at some time or other.

The religious authorities broke the commandment not to bear false witness. They were afraid the Romans would destroy their temple and so they put the true temple to death on a cross, fulfilling Jesus's prophetic word: '*Destroy this temple, and in three days I will raise it up' (John 2v19)*. Jesus was speaking of the temple of his body.

False witness is the theft of reputation and may well lead to the theft of life, as we have seen. It is often motivated by jealousy or envy.

Again Stephen says, '*And the patriarchs, jealous of Joseph, sold him into Egypt ...' (Acts 7v9)*.

THE TENTH COMMANDMENT

> *You shall not covet your neighbour's house; you shall not covet your neighbour's wife, or his manservant, or his maidservant, or his ox, or his ass, or anything that is your neighbour's. (Exodus 20v17).*

Coveting had a major part to play in original sin – the first sin committed in the Garden of Eden. Genesis 3v6:

So when the woman saw that the tree was good for food, and that it was a delight to the eyes, and that the tree was to be desired to make one wise... she desired it, although God had expressly forbidden it.

The sin of Achan involved coveting. *'When I saw among the spoil a beautiful mantle from Shinar... then I coveted them, and took them...'* (*Joshua 7v21*).

The sin of Miriam and Aaron, the siblings of Moses, involved their coveting his position as leader: *'Has the Lord indeed spoken only through Moses? Has he not spoken through us also?' (Numbers 12v2).*

David coveted Bathsheba, Uriah's wife. Ahab coveted Naboth's vineyard (1 Kings 21v1).

Coveting is idolatry. *Be sure of this, that no fornicator or impure man, or one who is covetous (that is, an idolater), has any inheritance in the kingdom of Christ and of God (Ephesians 5v5).*

Coveting is a wrong desire, or a desire for the wrong things. It is desiring those things that belong to another. It is a sinful obsession. Satan offered Eve something that did not belong to him.

Achan coveted things given to God – things which belonged to God, which God had set apart for destruction. Achan's sin led to many lives being lost in the next battle (Joshua 7). Eve's coveting led to the fall of the whole human race.

King Ahab coveted Naboth's vineyard. However, Naboth would not compromise over his vineyard because he did not have the right to sell it. The land was covenanted by God to Naboth and to his family forever. Naboth was a righteous man living in ungodly times, and his refusal to sell his vineyard to King Ahab resulted in him being falsely accused and then murdered (1 Kings 21).

Covetousness leads to a miserly spirit; it may lead to withholding a gift or a tithe, or giving with a grudging spirit. Those who hold back suffer want (Proverbs 11v24–25). This proverb looks at the generous man who is enriched, not just with wealth but within his heart. He is given wealth because he can be trusted by God to use it unselfishly. By contrast, the man who withholds grain in times of famine, waiting for the market to drive the price higher, is cursed by the people (Proverbs 11v26).

Covetousness is greed. Liberality is the antithesis of covetousness. It could even be described as the remedy, or the preventative medicine. An attitude of gratitude and contentment will also help to overcome this sin (Hebrews 13v5).

Paul tells us that he has learnt to be content, whatever his circumstances. *Not that I complain of want; for I have learned, in whatever state I am, to be content (Philippians 4v11).* The way he expresses it shows that it is not something that comes easily. We learn contentment through our experience, and our dealings with God.

Desire per se is not wrong. In 1 Corinthians 14v1 we are told to earnestly desire the spiritual gifts. Why is this acceptable? God wants all Christians to have them, and they are his to give and ours to ask for. Spiritual gifts are given for the service of others and for the glory of God. They are not for our glory, nor to make us wealthy.

In Acts 8 we have the account of Simon the magician who desired the power to anoint people with the Holy Spirit. He offered Peter money for this gift. His coveting was wickedness. Simon's attitude was of the flesh. He probably thought, 'If only I had these powers then people would worship, admire and applaud me.' He may not have specifically identified worship as one of his desires, for this temptation is subtle, but it equates to wanting glory, wanting worship and seeking attention for himself. He had what could only be described as an Absalomic spirit. This desire for power, fame and celebrity, which is achieved by acquiring a gift, is what Absalom sought: he wanted David's throne (2 Samuel 15v1–12).

Simon, in turn, wanted the Son of David's throne. This use of a gift to achieve or enhance celebrity status, to become an idol or an object of worship, and thereby hold sway over others and obtain untold wealth, is dangerous.

Peter points out how serious his coveting is by saying to Simon, *'Repent therefore of this wickedness of yours, and pray to the Lord that, if possible, the intent of your heart may be forgiven you. For I see that you are in the gall of bitterness and in the bond of iniquity.' (Acts 8v22–23).*

Covetousness can lead to deceit. In Acts 5v1–11, we see that Ananias and his wife Sapphira lied to the Holy Spirit. Ananias and Sapphira had privately promised to God the proceeds from the sale of a piece of property. Nobody knew about this vow that they had made, and no one knew how much money they had raised through the sale. They could not resist holding back some of the proceeds for themselves. They obviously thought that no one would discover their sin. They believed that they would still get all the kudos for their generosity, but the Holy Spirit revealed to Peter what they had done. Their sin was exposed; they were not generous-spirited givers. They were mean-hearted givers.

Chapter Five

Judas Iscariot, a Man Trying to Make Amends

Judas Iscariot was one of the twelve men appointed to be with Jesus. He was the one who betrayed Jesus Christ for thirty pieces of silver. When he saw the consequence of what he had done he was filled with remorse. He became burdened by the enormity of his sin. What could he do to deal with this? He felt he needed to do something significant, so he came up with the final solution, the ultimate price – he gave his life to deal with his guilt. He went out and hanged himself.

Why did he betray Jesus? He was angry and bitter at having been exposed by Jesus. Jesus had sided with a woman whom he had accused of squandering valuable ointment when she anointed Jesus. In Judas's view this was a waste of money. In John 12v1–11 we have an account of this event where Mary, the sister of Lazarus and Martha, anoints Jesus. We are told that a beautiful aroma filled the house, representing her unashamedly public praise, thanksgiving and worship of Jesus. This act of love was expensive. It was lavish. It was, indeed, a profuse outpouring of a most costly sacrifice. However, it was resented by this covetous disciple who had control of the cash box. He was the treasurer and had position, power and prestige. Perhaps he thought he was going to be the Chancellor of the Exchequer in the new kingdom of Jesus, but he was taking his cut. In his anger he went out and betrayed his master for money. He may have rationalised that this was compensation for loss of 'earnings'. Jesus states that the ointment was for his burial. One can easily imagine the risposte going through Judas's mind: 'You want a burial? Then I'll give you a burial.' Just as Cain was angry at God for exposing his sin, so Judas was angry at the Son of God for exposing him.

Why did Mary lavish this ointment on Jesus? Jesus had raised her brother Lazarus from the dead. He was worthy of her adoration and gratitude, and is worthy of ours too!

There are people who feel sorry for Judas. However, they forget, or do not realise, or perhaps do not believe the scriptures that tell us plainly that Judas was a thief. His reaction to the rebuke of Jesus shows how dangerous it is to hold on to our anger.

Be angry but do not sin; do not let the sun go down on your anger, and give no opportunity to the devil (Ephesians 4v26–27).

We are told that Satan, that is, the Devil, entered Judas Iscariot (Luke 22v3). This took place because he had held on to his anger. He had left himself open to the Devil's attack. We can say that the same thing happened with Cain, which then caused him to murder his brother. *The Lord said to Cain, 'Why are you angry, and why has your countenance fallen? If you do well, will you not be accepted? And if you do not do well, sin is crouching at the door; its desire is for you, but you must master it' (Genesis 4v6–7).*

Judas Iscariot had found himself in a position of utter hopelessness. He had made a very bad choice and was in despair, void of hope. There are times when people find themselves in such despair, albeit for different reasons. Peter, who denied Christ, went out and wept bitterly. He too plunged to the depths of despair. However, when Peter met and was forgiven by the risen Jesus, Peter's life was transformed. As long as we are alive there is hope for us, even if we think we have committed the unpardonable sin.

So, what should we do to atone for our sins?

Chapter Six

Cornelius, a Man who Revered God

Most people think that by doing good deeds they will get to heaven. This is a fallacy. If it were so then there would have been no need for Jesus to come to earth, become a man, die on the cross for our sins, and be gloriously raised from the dead.

The Bible tells us plainly that we are saved by grace, through faith, and not by our works (Ephesians 2v8–9). Let us consider for a moment an excellent man named Cornelius (Acts chapter 10). Cornelius was a Gentile, that is, a person who was not a Jew.

This is how he is further described:

- He was a centurion of the Italian cohort;
- He was a devout man who feared God;
- He gave alms liberally to the people;
- He prayed constantly to God.

Here is a man who appears to be good; surely his good deeds and his prayerfulness will get him straight into heaven. It will not. One day he has a vision in which he is told by an angel to send for the apostle Peter.

Peter has a problem with visiting a Gentile, but as he argues with God he sees sense, repents, and goes to meet Cornelius. We pick up the account in Acts 11v13–14.

Cornelius recounts to Peter, his travelling companions and his household, how he had a vision and was instructed by an angel of God to send for Peter. The angel said '… *Peter will declare to you a message by which you will be saved, you and all your household' (Acts 11v14).*

God had been doing a work in Cornelius and had brought him to a point where he was ready to receive the gospel. We note, quite clearly, that he was not yet saved. It is by hearing the gospel that we are saved. The apostle Paul says, '*So faith comes from what is heard, and what is heard comes by the preaching of Christ' (Romans 10v17).*

The gospel is the means by which we are saved. The good works of Cornelius were not adequate. We would consider him to be a good man, and so he was. It also shows that the caption on a leaflet published by the organisation 'Jews for Jesus' is true: 'You do not have to be Jewish to believe in Jesus.' Cornelius was not Jewish, but he came to believe in Jesus through the preaching of the gospel by a Jew named Peter.

Chapter Seven

Jonah, a Prophet
who Points us to Jesus

Jonah was a prophet of God who was sent on a mission to announce God's forthcoming judgement on Nineveh, the capital of Assyria. The short account of his mission appears in the Old Testament book of Jonah. He was a Hebrew, born in Israel, which had suffered greatly under the might of Assyria's barbaric war machine.

So God sent Jonah to warn Nineveh of its impending destruction. Why send a warning? Why not just go ahead and destroy Nineveh? God desires that all men repent and turn to him, and so he warns them (2 Peter 3v9). This is why we have the Bible to warn us of hell.

Jonah, however, wanted God to punish Israel's cruel enemies, and so he refused to go. In fact, he fled from the presence of God. However, the Bible tells us that God is omnipresent (Jeremiah 23v24; Psalm 139v7–16) and Jonah would have known this. What does it mean, therefore, to flee from God's presence? God chose to dwell in the midst of his people, Israel. The temple in Jerusalem was, so to speak, his official residence. Jonah was fleeing from Jerusalem. We also remember that Adam and Eve tried to hide from God's presence (Genesis 3v8–10).

Jonah fled to the port of Joppa and boarded a ship headed for Tarshish, as far away as possible from Jerusalem and Nineveh.

So how might we flee from God's presence? Some possibilities are to:

- avoid contact with God's people (the Church);
- avoid God's Word (the Bible).

To do this we persuade ourselves that:

- those who go to church are all hypocrites;
- science has disproved the Bible;
- most people do not go to church;
- we do not need to read the Bible.

The essence of flight from God is to avoid places where we think God might communicate with us.

So, Jonah is now sailing away to Tarshish and is below deck, sound asleep. *But the LORD hurled a great wind upon the sea, and there was a mighty tempest on the sea, so that the ship threatened to break up (Jonah 1v4).*

The sailors are terrified, each crying out to his god. The ship's captain finds Jonah, rouses him from his sleep and tells him to pray to his God. The crew know that unless something supernatural happens they are doomed. They then cast lots to see who is to blame, and the lot falls on

Jonah. What else would you expect? Proverbs 16v33 tells us: *The lot is cast into the lap, but the decision is wholly from the Lord.* God is in control! Did we ever think that man was great and in control of his destiny? If we still do, then this challenges our position and we will need to humble ourselves before God and recognise, as King Nebuchadnezzar did, that God is in control of the affairs of men (Daniel 4).

The sailors interrogate Jonah and discover that he is a Hebrew fleeing from the presence of God – the God who made the sea and dry land. They become exceedingly afraid because they now know that it is Jonah's fault, and that Jonah's God is all-powerful. They ask Jonah what they should do, and he tells them to throw him into the sea. We may wonder why he didn't just jump. A possible explanation is that God required them to identify with the sacrifice. At first the men will not throw Jonah overboard, for they are afraid to take human life. Then they try with all their might to row back to land, but the tempest just gets worse; the waves are mountainous. Desperate, they turn to prayer, calling out to the true and living God, the God of Jonah, for mercy. They do not call out to their own gods, because these gods had neither power nor authority. They were false! The sailors plead for their lives to be spared, and for forgiveness for taking the life of God's prophet, Jonah, recognising that God can do as he pleases. They were more concerned that God would punish them if they took his life.

When they finally throw Jonah into the sea, it immediately stops raging. Then these men fear the Lord and worship him with a sacrifice and vows.

What we see here is the prophetic enactment by Jonah of the idea that one man's life satisfies the wrath of God. God's rage against the sailors ceased. They were awed, and worshipped the true God. The Lord became their God.

When Jesus died on the cross, the wrath of God toward man was satisfied. It all fell on Jesus. We are safe. We should worship and fear this God and make him our God. There is no other God, and he alone is worthy of our worship.

We are not told what vows these men made, but they were obviously vows to God. Men often make vows to God in a crisis. Recalling the terror of war, it has been said: *There are no atheists in foxholes.*

However, in this case, we note that these men made their promises post-crisis! They were grateful to God for his mercy. We can conclude that they made vows to serve this God, the living God. Their own gods did not deliver them from their doom. Only the God of heaven and earth could do this.

Now consider this: only Christ can save us from hell. We should therefore accept the sacrifice of Christ: one man dying for the sins of the world, thus appeasing the wrath of God toward us. We should make our vows to him alone, to serve him for the rest of our lives in gratitude for what he has done for us. We must jettison false gods and serve the true God.

Jonah was now dead. He had drowned before he was swallowed by a whale. He remained for three days and three nights in its belly. Jesus too was entombed for three days. Jonah was to be a sign to the men of Nineveh, as Jesus was to be to his generation (Luke 11v30). God had mercy on Jonah, raised him from the dead and gave him a second chance (Jonah 3v1). Note, however, that the task does not change; Jonah is still sent to Nineveh. He is sent to proclaim a message in this city. The message was simple: *'Yet forty days, and Nineveh shall be overthrown!'* (*Jonah 3v4*).

It does not seem to be much of a message. We may ask questions about this. Is this all he said? Did he deliver the message accurately? Yes, and it was enough; he would not have dared to change it. There is power in God's Word, and it needs nothing more than the Holy Spirit to bring new life (Ezekiel 37).

Seeing Jonah alive after he was known to have died spoke volumes to the people; it confirmed that judgement was coming, just as the resurrection of Jesus confirms that judgement is coming to us (Acts 17v31). It is most likely that the account of the voyage to Tarshish would have travelled to Nineveh, affirming the death of Jonah and the impact of his sacrificial death.

How much warning will God give us before he calls us to account? Like the people of Nineveh, we have already been given a warning. The simple gospel message is the power of God for salvation. You will have heard of the resurrection of Jesus which confirms the judgement hanging over you. It is my sincere hope that you have been gripped by what you have heard.

What should we do then? Believe the gospel. Put our trust in the death of Christ on the cross, believing that his death has paid the penalty for our sin and appeased the wrath of God. The gospel is simple, as the Philippian gaoler discovered: *'Believe in the Lord Jesus, and you will be saved'* *(Acts 16v31).*

There is power indeed in God's Word:

- Creative power – *And God said, 'Let there be light'; and there was light (Genesis 1);*
- Redemptive power – *For I am not ashamed of the gospel: it is the power of God for salvation … (Romans 1v16);*

- Convicting power – *For the word of God is living and active ... and discerning the thoughts and intentions of the heart (Hebrews 4v12);*
- Praying power – The Lord's Prayer: *Our Father, who art in heaven, hallowed be thy name ... (Matthew 6v9–14).*

We have seen how Jonah points to Jesus. In the following chapters we will consider Jesus himself.

Chapter Eight

Who is Jesus?
The Testimony of John

We need to turn our attention to Jesus Christ and consider:

- who he is;
- what he did.

In the Bible we have the four Gospels, namely, Matthew, Mark, Luke and John. These record for us eye-witness accounts of the life, death and resurrection of Jesus Christ. When we read through the Gospels in the Bible they challenge us to answer the question, 'Who is Jesus?' We need to answer this question for ourselves and, while we will look at some of the Gospel accounts in brief here, it is important that readers examine the Gospels for themselves. As you do so, ask God to give you understanding of his Word.

In order to whet the reader's appetite we will take a brief look at the Gospel of John, adding, where relevant, further details from other Bible passages, in particular, from the testimony of Moses.

Imagine for a moment that you are in a court room where:

- there is a trial taking place;
- Jesus is in the dock;
- John is the defence barrister;
- John has various witnesses to call;
- we are the jury.

In the first chapter John sets out what he intends to show the court. He will show that Jesus is God and that he became a man. He will then call witnesses to testify about Jesus: his identity, his purpose and his actions. Furthermore, he will present us with a variety of evidence based on some of the signs Jesus performed, together with various encounters he had with people, and interlaced with Jesus's own testimony.

WHO IS JOHN?

John had been a disciple of John the Baptist before he followed Jesus (John 1v35–38). It was John the Baptist who pointed John to Jesus. John was a fisherman, as was his brother James. Both were ambitious men wanting top positions in Christ's kingdom (Matthew 20v20–24).

He had a rather quaint way of referring to himself as 'the disciple whom Jesus loved'. Perhaps John was self-effacing. There is another aspect here: Jesus had an unusual style of referring to himself in the third person, e.g. '...*the Son can do nothing of his own accord, but only what he sees the Father doing*' (*John 5v19*). This suggests that John may have been following the style of Jesus because of his admiration for him.

JOHN'S OPENING REMARKS

In the beginning was the Word, and the Word was with God, and the Word was God. He was in the beginning with God; all things were made through him, and without him was not anything made that was made (John 1v1–3).

We may ask, 'Who is the Word?' John tells us that Jesus is the Word: *And the Word became flesh and dwelt among us … (John 1v14).*

John asserts that Jesus was *in the beginning.* He was not a created being: he existed prior to creation. Indeed, he was instrumental in the creation of the heavens and the earth. He was in the beginning with God, that is, God the Father and, indeed, John tells us that Jesus *is* God. John tells us that God the Son took on human flesh and lived among people. In other words, God became a man.

JOHN'S PURPOSE IN WRITING HIS GOSPEL

Why does John relate all this? He explains his purpose towards the end of the Gospel in John 20v30–31: *Now Jesus did many other signs in the presence of the disciples, which are not written in this book; but these are written that you may believe that Jesus is the Christ, the Son of God, and that believing you may have life in his name.*

His purpose, then, is for the readers of his Gospel to receive eternal life. Jesus himself tells us what eternal life is: *And this is eternal life, that they know thee the only true God, and Jesus Christ whom thou hast sent (John 17v3).* It is to have a personal relationship with God, to *know* God and not merely to *know about* God. To enter into a personal relationship with God, the barrier to such a relationship must be dealt with first. That barrier is called 'sin': … *but your iniquities have made a separation between you and your God, and your sins have hid his face from you so that he does not hear (Isaiah 59v2).*

To achieve his purpose John sets out to show who Jesus is and what he did. He gives an account of the words of Jesus, some of the events in his short life on earth, and some of the reactions of people to him. John does not tell us about his birth, but Matthew and Luke do so in their Gospels.

John writes his Gospel so that:

- we may believe that Jesus is the Son of God;
- in believing we may have eternal life in his name.

John testifies that what he has seen and reported is the truth. He wants the hearer to believe his account. He is emphatic that he is telling the truth: *He who saw it has borne witness – his testimony is true, and he knows that he tells the truth – that you also may believe (John 19v35).*

Now, if we do not want to believe the words of Jesus recorded for us as evidence, we are also given an account of some of the signs Jesus did so that we may consider them, and believe because of them: *'If I am not doing the works of my Father, then do not believe me; but if I do them, even though you do not believe me, believe the works, that you may know and understand that the Father is in me and I am in the Father' (John 10v37–38).*

> *'But the testimony which I have is greater than that of John; for the works which the Father has granted me to accomplish, these very works which I am doing, bear me witness that the Father has sent me' (John 5v36).*

Having considered John's background and his purpose in writing, let us move on to examine the evidence that he presents. Firstly we will turn our attention to the people Jesus encountered, and then to the signs that he performed.

JOHN THE BAPTIST (John 1v19–36)

John the Baptist's very purpose was to reveal Jesus to Israel (John 1v31). He met Jesus at Bethany and testified that Jesus was the Lamb of God who takes away the sin of the world (John 1v29, 36). The blood of Jesus atones for our sins and appeases the wrath of God. The word 'atone' means simply to make at one or to reconcile. It is his blood that pays the penalty for our sins, so that we may be reconciled to God. Jesus is the true Passover lamb without blemish, that is, sinless and without a bone broken (Exodus 12v46). All households had to eat the Passover lamb and apply its blood to the doorposts (Exodus 12v13).

The blood of Christ needs to be applied by faith to our lives lest we perish. The angel of death did not smite the firstborn in houses which had the blood on the doorposts. When God sees the blood of his Son applied by faith to our lives, we will not suffer eternal damnation but have eternal life.

Jesus is the Son of God (John 1v34), the one who baptises with the Holy Spirit rather than with water (John 1v33). John had seen God the Holy Spirit descend as a dove from heaven and remain on Jesus. This, in fact, had been the sign that God the Father had given to John the Baptist to identify the Messiah, the Son of God (John 1v33).

NICODEMUS (John 3)

John, through Jesus's encounter with Nicodemus, brings in the testimony of Moses. Here is what we learn from this encounter:

- We must be born again to see and enter the kingdom of God (John 3v3, 5, 7);
- Whoever puts his trust in Jesus will have eternal life (John 3v14–16);
- God loves the world and does not want it to perish (John 3v17);
- God sacrificed his Son to procure eternal life for us (John 3v16);
- He who does not believe is already condemned (John 3v18).

The death of Christ, who was lifted up on the cross, was foreshadowed in Moses's day by the incident of the bronze serpent, with the requirement for faith in God's Word.

Nicodemus was afraid to approach Jesus publicly, for he was a member of the council – a Pharisee. His reputation and his position would have been threatened (John 7v50). He was a teacher of Israel (John 3v10).

Jesus told the Jews that Moses had borne witness to him. Although they, like Nicodemus, had studied the writings of Moses carefully, they showed their unbelief by rejecting Jesus. Moses had written prophetically about Jesus (John 5v39–47) in his accounts of the Passover, the bronze serpent and the manna.

The manna was known as the bread from heaven which God gave the Israelites to eat while they dwelt for forty years in the wilderness. Jesus claimed to be the true bread of God which came down from heaven and gives eternal life to the world (John 6v33–35). *'If you believed Moses, you would believe me, for he wrote of me' (John 5v46).*

John introduced Moses in John 1v45: *Philip found Nathanael, and said to him, 'We have found him of whom Moses in the law and also the prophets wrote, Jesus of Nazareth, the son of Joseph.'*

The testimony of Moses pointed prophetically to the means of salvation:

- The Passover Lamb (John 1v29, 35–36);
- The bronze serpent (John 3v14–15);
- The manna – the true bread which comes down from heaven (John 6v51).

We will look at the testimony of Moses, that is, his writings, in chapter 9.

OTHER ENCOUNTERS

Jesus encounters a woman at the well with the promise of the Holy Spirit described as *living water.* It is his prerogative to baptise with the Holy Spirit, as John the Baptist had testified, and so Jesus makes an assertion that he is the Son of God (John1v34). He tells this woman, *'If you knew the gift of God, and who it is that is saying to you, "Give me a drink", you would have asked him, and he would have given you living water'* *(John 4v10).* The impact that Jesus had on her is noteworthy. She had come to the well at noon to avoid people because of her lifestyle. She had been ashamed to be seen in public. This is why she asks Jesus for living water, so that she need not come to this public well again to draw water. Now she returns to her city and declares unashamedly that she thinks she may have found the Messiah. She herself was waiting for the Messiah (John 4v25). Jesus had told Nicodemus that he could not see the kingdom of God unless he was born anew. The word 'see' would indicate that someone has to look or be looking. Jesus reveals himself to those who are seeking him.

John's Gospel reports several other encounters Jesus had during his ministry with people such as Nicodemus. Sometimes signs and encounters come together: for example, Jesus encountered Martha when he brought her brother Lazarus back to life (John 11). He also reported some of the encounters the risen Jesus had with Mary Magdalene, Thomas (Doubting Thomas) and Peter.

SIGNS THAT JESUS PERFORMED

The signs are given to show that the Father has sent Jesus, and to glorify the Father and the Son (John 5v36; John 10v25–26).

Turning water into wine

Jesus manifests his glory, showing his power and authority over creation. John had already asserted that Jesus was the creator of the world. Turning water into wine was the first sign that Jesus performed (John 2v1-11). The wine at a wedding feast had run out, and Jesus's mother, Mary, reported this to him. Since he had not performed a miracle previously, it is not clear what Mary expected him to do. Jesus then turned water into wine.

Transformation of water had been performed centuries before, but with a less than pleasing result, as we read in the book of Exodus.

Moses, at God's command, turned the water of the River Nile into blood so that the Egyptians could not drink it. The purpose of this sign was to show Pharaoh and the Egyptians that there was a God to be reckoned with. God was making himself known to Egypt. This is how Moses recorded it in Exodus 7v17–18: *Thus says the Lord, 'By this you shall know that I am the Lord: behold, I will strike the water that is in the Nile with the rod that is in my hand, and it shall be turned to blood, and the fish in the Nile shall die, and the Nile shall become foul, and the Egyptians will loathe to drink water from the Nile.'*

We should note that in an earlier encounter with Moses, Pharaoh had said rather contemptuously, *'Who is the Lord, that I should heed his voice and let Israel go?' (Exodus 5v2).* The Lord was the God of the Hebrews whom Pharaoh had enslaved and who were powerless against the Egyptians. So here, in other words, is Pharaoh's verdict: 'I do not need to listen to or show respect to this God who is unable to deliver his people.' With hindsight we know just how wrong he was!

It may be that we see how the church is held in contempt and reviled these days, and conclude that God is powerless and that we will not be called to account by him. However, we should learn from what happened to Pharaoh, which is recorded for us as a merciful warning, and which we should heed.

So we see that God was making himself known to Pharaoh, Egypt and, of course, the Israelites (Exodus 10v1–2).

We see in John's Gospel a parallel: Jesus is making himself known by revealing his glory through his first sign. It shows that he has the power to transform his creation. We should note, too, the complimentary comments made by the steward of the feast when he remarks: '...*but you have kept the good wine until the last*' (*John 2v10*). He is observing that it is usual at wedding banquets for the good wine to be served first. Then, when the guests have drunk freely and are no longer able to discern quality, poor wine is served. Here the guests had already tasted the good wine. However, the steward was able to tell that this latter wine was far superior. What are we to make of this?

At this banquet we have good wine followed by even better wine. This, I believe, is an indication that the new creation is far superior to the first. The new creation is referred to in Nicodemus's encounter with Jesus, and comes about by the new birth.

However that is not all, for God's creation was made out of nothing (Hebrews 11v3). God created a vast expanse of water, out of which he formed solid ground (2 Peter 3v5). Water was turned into land. Some translations refer to this as a separation of land and water, implying that God had already created the solid ground.

We will not go into detail here because much has been written on creation by experts in the field. What we will note is that the earth was made out of water, that is, water was turned into earth. So when Jesus turns water into wine, this sign informs us that Jesus is creator of the heavens, and the earth and everything in it. It is a clear indication of his identity. Turning water into wine is an amazing sign. John commences his Gospel by stating that in the beginning was the Word, and that all things were created by the Word. It is no wonder that John starts his Gospel this way since the first miracle Jesus performed was a work of creation, transforming water into wine.

Forgiving sins

There was a man at the Bethesda pool who had been ill for thirty-eight years. His illness and incapacity were due to his sin (John 5v14). Jesus healed him, and this healing demonstrated that the man had been forgiven. When we sin, we sin against God. Therefore it is God alone who has the right to forgive sin.

Furthermore, Jesus healed the man on the Sabbath day. The religious authorities were upset by this supposed breaking of the Sabbath, but Jesus upset them further when he claimed to be the Son of God, making himself equal with God (John 5v18). They considered this to be blasphemy and for this they sought to kill Jesus, not for one moment considering whether the claim of Jesus might be true.

What if it is true? Do we ever stop to consider this?

Are we so busy with our lives that we push aside the claims of Jesus?

Do we ever consider that we might be wrong about Jesus, damning him with our faint praise when we say that he was a good man, or a good teacher, or a wonderful example for humanity to follow, or a prophet, but no more than that?

In this account the authority of Jesus to forgive sins is implicit. We can deduce it from the words of Jesus in John 5v14: *'See, you are well! Sin no more, that nothing worse befall you.'* The implication is that his sin was the cause of his condition, and that if he continued in this sin something worse might happen to him. Thirty-eight years is a very long time to be ill! (John 5v5).

It would be wrong to think that all sickness results from a particular sin. In the account of the blind man Jesus firmly rejected the idea that all illness is caused by sin (John 9v1–3).

There is an explicit reference to Jesus's power to forgive sin in Mark 2v1–12. We read of a paralysed man being carried on a stretcher by four of his friends to Jesus. There was a large crowd preventing the men from gaining access to Jesus, but the four friends persisted, with great determination and resourcefulness. They climbed the exterior stairs and lowered the paralytic, on his stretcher, through the roof, before Jesus. Why? They had great compassion for their friend and believed that Jesus could heal him. They had faith in Jesus.

Even more astonishing than the commotion they caused by this dramatic entry was the response of Jesus, who said to the paralytic, *'My son, your sins are forgiven' (Mark 2v5).*

This raises an authentic question in the minds and hearts of the scribes: *'Why does this man speak thus? It is blasphemy! Who can forgive sins but God alone?' (Mark 2v7).* Clearly they had dismissed the possibility that Jesus was God, in spite of all the evidence of his miracles in the local area. They rightly stated that only God can forgive sins.

Sin against God

When we sin, we sin against God, though it is true that others may also suffer. When King David had been exposed for committing adultery with Bathsheba, and then murdering her husband, Uriah, (2 Samuel 11v1–17), he says to God, *'Against thee, thee only, have I sinned, and done that which is evil in thy sight' (Psalm 51v4).*

How can this be so? What sin had he committed?

To begin with, he had broken four of the Ten Commandments:

- You shall not covet;
- You shall not steal;
- You shall not commit adultery;
- You shall not kill.

Essentially King David had shown unbelief and contempt for the Word of God (2 Samuel 11v4, 15). His actions showed that not believing God's Word matters. He had disobeyed God. He may not have considered it explicitly, but his actions certainly showed that he thought that God would not see him. Uriah was one of David's 'mighty men'; he was a Hittite who risked his life in David's service. Perhaps David had shown contempt for this foreigner who had allied himself to God's people.

Will God not see or care? See how the writer answers this question in Psalm 94v1–11:

> *O LORD, thou God of vengeance,*
> *thou God of vengeance, shine forth!*
> *Rise up, O judge of the earth;*
> *render to the proud their deserts!*
> *O LORD, how long shall the wicked,*
> *how long shall the wicked exult?*
> *They pour out their arrogant words,*
> *they boast, all the evildoers.*
> *They crush thy people, O LORD,*
> *and afflict thy heritage.*
> *They slay the widow and the sojourner,*

and murder the fatherless;
and they say, 'The LORD does not see;
the God of Jacob does not perceive.'
Understand, O dullest of the people!
Fools, when will you be wise?
He who planted the ear, does he not hear?
He who formed the eye, does he not see?
He who chastens the nations, does he not chastise?
He who teaches men knowledge,
the Lord, knows the thoughts of man,
that they are but a breath.

We cannot hide our sin from God. To think that God does not see or hear is folly, since it was he who gave us hearing, and sight, and minds to think for ourselves. He knows what we think and say.

Proof of sins forgiven

Some Christians suggest that Jesus believed that our greatest need is forgiveness of sins, and not healing. They are right in saying this. However, I think it is incorrect to conclude that Jesus forgave the paralysed man his sins, but did not heal him at the same time. They maintain that Jesus healed the paralytic afterwards as a separate miracle, to authenticate his power and authority to forgive sins.

I think that to view the events of this miracle through such a filter leads to a misunderstanding of what actually happened. We might think that Jesus could have shown that he had the authority to forgive sins by exercising his power to heal.

Firstly, we need to take note that his power to heal was widely known already. He had healed others prior to this, including Simon Peter's mother-in-law (Mark 1v30–31). He had cast out an unclean spirit in the Capernaum synagogue and, subsequently, the whole town had brought their sick to him. Then here he is again in Capernaum uttering the words: *'Your sins are forgiven' (Mark 2v5)*.

Secondly, we need to ask the appropriate question. In this context, it is not relevant to ask, 'Does Jesus have power to heal this man?' The question we should be asking is, 'How can we know that this man's sins are forgiven?' The healing per se does not tell us anything about the man's spiritual state.

What, then, are we to conclude here?

We conclude that this is a case where the illness is the result of some specific sin, and that if the sin, which caused the illness, is dealt with then the illness will go.

The healing took place immediately Jesus forgave the paralytic his sins. This raises the question, 'Why did he not move when he was healed?'

What would we have done? The man just lay there listening to Jesus, waiting for the command to get up. He was just as transfixed as we might have been.

Jesus then told him to get up and go home. The fact that the man did exactly that showed that he had been healed. It is the way we know his sins had been forgiven, for they had been the direct cause of his paralysis.

It is worth reiterating that not all sickness is a direct result of a specific sin. In John 9v1–3 Jesus says of a blind man that it was neither his sin nor that of his parents that caused his blindness.

Feeding the five thousand

Jesus is the true bread come down from heaven (John 6v32, 48–51). If you want eternal life you must eat of him, that is, partake by faith. He is the bread of God (Leviticus 22v25).

He fed five thousand people with just five loaves and two fish. Do we doubt this miracle? We are going to be asked to believe an even more incredible ratio than this, that of one life feeding the whole world. Jesus says that unless you eat his flesh and drink his blood, you have no life in you. He is not, of course, speaking literally here, that is, he is not talking about cannibalism. We can take our cue from an earlier chapter where Jesus responds to Nicodemus on the question of new birth. Nicodemus did us a favour by asking this crucial question: *'How can a man be born when he is old? Can he enter a second time into his mother's womb and be born?' (John 3v4).* The new birth is not physical; it is spiritual.

So what do we do when we eat? We partake of life-giving, life-sustaining substances. Eating is the process by which we consume food and sustain life.

To eat the flesh of Jesus and to drink his blood is to partake of him. This is the means by which he gives us life, that is, eternal life. We do this by faith, believing his Word.

Giving sight to the man born blind

In John 9 we have the account of Jesus's encounter with a man who was born blind. His disciples raise a question concerning his blindness: was it his sin or his parents' sin that caused it? We have already considered cases where illness is caused by sin, for example, in the healing of the paralytic who was lowered through the roof by his friends, and the man at the pool of Bethesda. However, Jesus explains that this man's blindness was not caused by sin. Rather, it was given that the works of God might be displayed in him. Jesus gave him sight. This was done on the Sabbath day.

We may care to note that it is Jesus alone who gives sight to the spiritually blind. Looking back to Nicodemus, Jesus said: *'Unless one is born anew, he cannot see the kingdom of God' (John 3v3).* Nicodemus and Joseph of Arimathea were seeking the kingdom of God.

Jesus fulfils the prophecy of Isaiah 61 by giving sight to this blind man (John 9v3, 32). This is a very encouraging account for the Christian, for we witness a man being driven to faith in Christ by those who hated Christ. They began persecuting this man rather than rejoicing with him because he had received sight. The account demonstrates that faith is logical, and that opposition to Christ is irrational and fuelled by jealousy and hatred. It shows too that God's purpose cannot be thwarted. Here is a man minding his own business, going nowhere in life, and on this day Jesus heals him, and all of a sudden he is caught up in a maelstrom of persecution. The man is taken to the Pharisees, who ask him how he received his sight. He tells them that Jesus had healed him. Some of them conclude that Jesus was not from God because he had healed the man on the Sabbath (John 9v16). Others say, 'How can a sinner do such signs?' Then they ask the man his opinion of Jesus. He tells them that Jesus is a prophet.

They seek evidence of his previous blindness, questioning whether he had really been blind and whether a miracle had even taken place. His parents confirm that he was born blind and had been blind up to this very day, but they are afraid to give their opinion of Jesus. Why were the Pharisees so concerned about this miracle that they wanted to disprove it? No one born blind had been given sight before, and it demonstrated clearly that Jesus had power to heal; this backed his claim to be the Son of God.

Then the Pharisees question the man again. He will not be drawn on opinions but says what he knows: that he was once blind but that now he can see. Still the Pharisees persist with their questioning.

Let us look at the man's interaction with the religious authorities.

He gets impatient: 'Why do you want to know? Do you too want to become his disciples?' What a marvellous riposte, and how courageous of the man!

They revile him, saying: *'You are his disciple, but we are disciples of Moses. We know that God has spoken to Moses, but as for this man, we do not know where he comes from' (John 9v28–29).*

In John 9v30–33 we follow his thought process: *The man answered, 'Why, this is a marvel! You do not know where he comes from, and yet he opened my eyes. We know that God does not listen to sinners, but if any one is a worshipper of God and does his will, God listens to him. Never since the world began has it been heard that any one opened the eyes of a man born blind. If this man were not from God, he could do nothing.'*

The Pharisees answered him, *'You were born in utter sin, and would you teach us?' And they cast him out (John 9v34).*

Afterwards Jesus sought him out and made himself known to the man, and he believed in Jesus and worshipped Jesus.

He is being forced to think about Jesus, and we see how he is drawing his own conclusion that Jesus is from God: that Jesus is not a sinner, and that God listens to Jesus. He was not actually teaching them; rather, he was teaching himself the truth about Jesus. They, on the other hand, were unteachable. It shows the logic of faith: we see that unbelief denies the blindingly obvious, and leads to irrational and petty behaviour. One minute they are saying he was never blind, and the next minute they are saying that he was born in utter sin, implying that his former blindness provides proof. We see a man's theology developing in adverse terrain, and in the cauldron of pressure. We are given the privilege of observing this man's thinking, courtesy of Satan's agents. We see how Satan can drive a man to faith.

The Pharisees accused him of being born in utter sin, claiming that this was the cause of his blindness. Jesus had already refuted this in his response to his disciples when they had asked about the cause of his blindness (John 9v1–3).

What are we to learn from this occasion? Jesus also opens the eyes of those who are born spiritually blind. Most people are not born physically blind, but all are born spiritually blind, and we need Jesus to give us sight. Here is a simple prayer by which we can ask for this spiritual sight: *Open my eyes, that I may behold wondrous things out of thy law (Psalm 119v18).*

Raising Lazarus from the dead

In John 11 we have the account of Jesus raising Lazarus from the dead – four days after he had died. Lazarus had two sisters.

We will observe how each of the three siblings has a role:

- Martha has a significant encounter with Jesus;
- Lazarus prophesies, graphically, the death and resurrection of Jesus;
- Mary anoints the feet of Jesus for burial.

We have seen that John has already picked up on encounters, as well as signs. Think of:

- Nicodemus (John 3);
- the Samaritan woman at the well (John 4);
- the man born blind (John 9).

However, the Gospel of John is not just about signs; it is also about significant encounters that Jesus had with various individuals. An encounter with Jesus is the most significant event that can take place in our lives.

Would you like to have an encounter with Jesus?

One day you will. We all will, after we die. We will stand before him, and he will judge us. It is far better to encounter him now and make peace with him.

John 11v35 is a familiar verse to many people, who often use it as an oath. The verse is very short, containing just two words which powerfully express the compassion of Jesus. The verse simply states: *Jesus wept.*

In March 1993 my father died. Several months before this I had been reading Psalm 119, and it was verse 136 that caught my attention. Here David says, *'My eyes shed streams of tears, because men do not keep thy law.'* My immediate thought was that I do not shed tears. Then, when my father died, my tears flowed profusely; restraint proved impossible. Later I reflected on why my tears had been so profuse. I had seen death before and had been able to contain my grief. This time it was different. Two reasons occurred to me:

- This was the closest loss that I had suffered;
- My mother's grief impacted on me.

The second reason may have been the more significant. I mention this because in the account we are about to consider, it may help us to understand why Jesus wept.

How often are we moved?

Are we moved when we see the lawlessness and idolatry so rife in society today? Paul was moved when he walked around Athens: ...*his spirit was provoked within him as he saw that the city was full of idols (Acts 17v16)*. Why should an idolatrous Gentile city bother a Jew? It bothered him because God did not appear to rule there. God's authority had been rejected.

The raising of Lazarus – a few observations

Lazarus was ill as we begin the account (John 11v1).

His sisters, Mary and Martha, sent word to Jesus informing him that their brother was ill (John 11v3).

They were waiting for Jesus to come and heal Lazarus. This, by the way, is an example of prayer or, more precisely, intercession. We plead with God on behalf of others. Am I saying that Jesus is God? Yes! The Gospel of John demands of us to know who Jesus is. As we read it we are forced to consider who Jesus is. However, only God the Holy Spirit can reveal this to us.

Note the simplicity of their intercession: they merely inform Jesus that Lazarus is ill. They expect Jesus to come and heal Lazarus. Note also how they attempt to use leverage with their words: *'Lord, he whom you love is ill' (John 11v3),* that is, if you really love Lazarus, and us, you will come and heal him immediately.

The illness was for the glory of God, and for Jesus to be glorified by means of it. Indeed, Martha will later give Jesus honour when she says, *'Lord, if you had been here, my brother would not have died' (John 11v21),* acknowledging his power to heal.

John tells us that Jesus loved Martha, Mary and Lazarus, so after hearing the news of Lazarus's illness he stayed two days longer where he was, before setting off for Bethany (John 11v5-6). We may think that this was a strange way for Jesus to show his love.

Jesus set off with his disciples for Bethany knowing full well that:

- The Jews had tried to kill him the last time he was there;
- Lazarus was already dead;
- He was risking his life for Lazarus.

Why did Lazarus die? Lazarus was, unwittingly, a prophet. Prophets were often called upon to enact a future event; for example, Ezekiel was told by God to lie on his side for 390 days and then a further 40 days. This was to represent the punishments to be meted out by God on Israel and Judah (Ezekiel 4v1–17). A reading of Ezekiel 4 will tell us of the suffering that Ezekiel had to undergo to show what would happen to God's people. Ezekiel was the message. Likewise Jonah became the message, as we saw in chapter 7.

So, what was Lazarus portraying and foretelling? He was acting out the death, burial and resurrection of our Lord Jesus Christ.

Jonah's death went further: one man was thrown into the sea to save the lives of the ship's crew. As soon as Jonah hit the sea the tempest ceased. God brought it to a halt. His wrath was quenched by this sacrifice. One man died for many men, foretelling how God would save the world. The ship's crew did not like the idea of Jonah dying for them.

Jonah being brought back to life confirmed to the people of Nineveh that God's judgement of them was certain, just as the resurrection of Jesus guarantees that God's judgement of us is certain. That certainty should alarm us.

In John 11v36 we are told why Jesus wept. Jesus loved Lazarus, but we are also told this in verse 5, where Jesus is said to love Martha, Mary and Lazarus. He wept because of what Lazarus had to go through – illness and suffering – and perhaps for what Lazarus would go through later: persecution and a death threat. He wept because of the sorrow of Martha and Mary, even though he knew he would soon bring Lazarus back to life. There is no shame in grief. It is right and proper to grieve, to shed tears, even though some may criticise such a display of emotion.

Jesus restores Lazarus to life. Who is this that has power over death? How does he conquer death? (Hebrews 2v14).

We know that Lazarus will live on and then die again, perhaps quite soon if the religious authorities have their way, for they sought to kill him because they envied Jesus, and their hatred of him grew as his popularity grew. Many Jews believed in Jesus because he raised Lazarus from the dead. Wouldn't we?

The raising of Lazarus was not final, because he would die again physically. He did not have a near-death experience. He actually died. His body had been in the tomb for four days, and Martha told Jesus that there would be a strong odour in the tomb. Jesus restored him to life. It was for Jesus's glory. The raising of Lazarus from death to life was a prophetic picture of the resurrection of Jesus. Lazarus was enacting a prophecy, and it was at considerable cost to him.

So, how can we be sure that we will be raised from the dead to eternal life? That is, how can we be sure of going to heaven when we die, thereby escaping eternal punishment? The answer is found in Jesus's conversation with Martha in John 11v25-26. The statement *he who believes in me* is the key. Jesus is *the resurrection and the life.* Resurrection and eternal life are found in Christ alone. If we trust in him alone, we will have eternal life.

The fact that Jesus promises that you will never die again is good news for those who will spend eternity in heaven. It indicates that those who go to hell will experience dying over and over again, without arriving at death or any end point where it can be said that it is finally over. So, the fact that we will not die physically a second time is not good news for those who will end up in hell.

I would not wish for anyone to experience this, and no one needs to! It is possible to be sure that once you die you will not experience the second death – in other words, it is possible to be certain that Jesus Christ will raise you to everlasting life. However, those who do not trust Christ will experience the second death, which is not a physical death like the first death, but everlasting torment.

So, how is this relevant for us?

Do we think that God has to account to us for all the injustices in the world? Are we failing to recognise the reality of our own situation – that God has the power to send us to hell, and that he would be justified in so doing. All of us are sinners and deserve to go to hell. We do not measure up to God's standard of righteousness.

When we are measured against that standard, which is Jesus Christ, we will be found lacking – a failure. The only way to go to heaven is to recognise this and have the righteousness of Jesus Christ made our own, that is, credited to our account.

His death on the cross paid the penalty for our sin. We do not have to pay the penalty ourselves; it would be unwise even to attempt it. His death has appeased the wrath of God, and his shed blood will cleanse us from our sin. Our own death cannot do this. Trusting in Jesus's death is our only hope. Any other sacrifice is blemished, and God will not accept us on the basis of a blemished sacrifice (Leviticus 22v25).

The resurrection of Jesus (John 20)

Jesus reveals himself after he has risen, to:

- Mary Magdalene;
- The disciples (with the exception of Thomas);
- The disciples again, with Thomas present.

Mary Magdalene

Three times Mary says that they have taken away her Lord. She says this to:

- Peter and John (John 20v2);
- The angel (John 20v13);
- Jesus himself (John 20v15).

She did not believe that he was alive, but rather, she thought that someone had taken his body away and buried it in

another place. The empty tomb was insufficient evidence that
Jesus had risen from the dead. This is borne out by Matthew's
account of the chief priests and the Pharisees. Matthew tells
us how they asked Pilate for the tomb to be guarded:

> *Next day, that is, after the day of Preparation, the chief
> priests and the Pharisees gathered before Pilate and said,
> 'Sir, we remember how that impostor said, while he was still
> alive, "After three days I will rise again." Therefore order
> the sepulchre to be made secure until the third day, lest his
> disciples go and steal him away, and tell the people, "He
> has risen from the dead," and the last fraud will be worse
> than the first.' Pilate said to them, 'You have a guard of
> soldiers; go, make it as secure as you can.' So they went and
> made the sepulchre secure by sealing the stone and setting a
> guard (Matthew 27v62–66).*

> Matthew 28v11–15 tells us: *While they were going, behold,
> some of the guard went into the city and told the chief priests
> all that had taken place. And when they had assembled with
> the elders and taken counsel, they gave a sum of money to the
> soldiers and said, 'Tell people, "His disciples came by night
> and stole him away while we were asleep." And if this comes
> to the governor's ears, we will satisfy him and keep you out of
> trouble.' So they took the money and did as they were directed;
> and this story has been spread among the Jews to this day.*

The religious authorities had been concerned that the
disciples might steal the body and claim that Jesus had
risen as he said he would, on the third day. So they had
arranged for the tomb to be sealed and guarded. Yet in spite
of this, the tomb had become empty. Furthermore, it was
clear that Jesus's body had not been stolen. The religious

authorities and the guards were denying the resurrection, though they had more evidence of it than Jesus's followers. The guards had reported to them what had happened – what they had seen and heard. Their reaction was denial born of unbelief; their hearts were hardened.

What did the guards see? What did they hear?

Matthew tells us that they saw an angel descend from heaven, roll away the stone from the door of the tomb, and sit upon the stone (Matthew 28v2–4). The face of the angel was like lightning, his clothing was as white as snow, and the guards were terrified. They had also experienced an earthquake. They were witnesses to the conversation between the angel and the women (Mary Magdalene and Mary, the mother of James and Joseph), and heard the angel say, *'Do not be afraid; for I know that you seek Jesus who was crucified. He is not here; for he has risen, as he said. Come, see the place where he lay. Then go quickly and tell his disciples that he has risen from the dead ...'* (Matthew 28v5–7).

We know that the heart of Mary Magdalene was far from hard and yet the empty tomb was not enough to convince her that Jesus was alive. Her only concern was to find the body of her Lord and bury it with honour.

Peter and John now believed Mary Magdalene's statement that the body of Jesus had been removed (John 20v2,8). Peter and John went home; there was no indication in their behaviour that they believed that Jesus had risen from the dead.

Mary Magdalene was weeping because she presumed that someone had removed the body of Jesus; she did not believe that he had risen. All three would come to believe this later when they met the risen Lord.

After Peter and John had left the tomb Jesus appeared to Mary Magdalene, but she did not know it was Jesus. Supposing Jesus to be the gardener, she says to him, *'Sir, if you have carried him away, tell me where you have laid him, and I will take him away' (John 20v15)*. Jesus then reveals himself to Mary. A stunned Mary clings to him; what bewilderment and joy she must have felt! Jesus tells her not to hold him, but to go and tell the disciples that he was ascending to his Father. He gives his disciples an opportunity for faith, to believe Mary's testimony – that he was alive. She obeys Jesus.

This, indeed, is the opportunity we ourselves are presented with: that is, to believe the testimonies of the disciples as recorded in the New Testament (John 20v24–25).

The disciples (except Thomas)

Jesus then appeared to the disciples when they were staying in a house. The doors were locked because they were afraid of the Jewish authorities. In spite of the physical barrier of the locked doors, Jesus entered and stood among them and said 'Peace be with you.' He showed them his hands and his side. Then they were glad when they saw the Lord. They reported all this to Thomas. However, Thomas did not believe their testimony.

Thomas and the other disciples

Thomas had responded to the testimony of the other disciples with three demands for evidence:

- To see the nail prints in the hands of Jesus;
- To put his finger in the mark of the nails;
- To place his hand in the side of Jesus where the mark from the spear would be.

Eight days later Jesus appeared to the disciples, and this time Thomas was present. Jesus rebuked Thomas for his unbelief and showed him each item of evidence he had sought. He told Thomas to touch the nail prints and feel the mark in his side where the spear had been thrust by the Roman soldier (John 19v34). We may wonder whether Thomas did actually touch the wounds of Jesus. I would suggest that he did because Jesus gave him an order and he would have obeyed!

Once Thomas's doubts had been removed he responded to Jesus by saying, *'My Lord and my God!' (John 20v28).*

We are generous to Thomas in speaking of his 'doubts', because this was unbelief. Our generosity stems from the sure knowledge that we would have done the same. Perhaps you would not have, but I think I and many others would have.

We should note here that Jesus was raised with a physical body. When John, in the opening verses of his first letter (1 John 1v1–4), speaks of seeing, hearing and touching Jesus, he would be referring, not just to the time they spent with him during his years of earthly ministry, but also to the time they had with him after his resurrection.

The resurrection demonstrates Christ's authority to judge

Jesus rose from the dead and made himself known to his disciples in accordance with scripture (John 20v9) and his Word. This is what John is telling us. Jesus is alive. The religious authorities were keen to ensure that the tomb was sealed up to and including the third day; no more was necessary, for if Jesus had risen on the fourth day that would have disproved his claims and made him a liar.

John tells us that the disciples recalled Jesus's words about raising up the destroyed temple in three days: *When therefore he was raised from the dead, his disciples remembered that he had said this; and they believed the scripture and the word which Jesus had spoken (John 2v22).*

The resurrection is a sign; it is the fulfilment of Jesus's words: *'Destroy this temple, and in three days I will raise it up' (John 2v19).* In John 2v18–22 the Jews ask Jesus for a sign to prove that he has the authority to cleanse the temple. The sign that he gave to the Jews was that they would destroy the temple, meaning his body, by putting him to death, and he would raise it up again within three days. If he has the power over death then he has the right to cleanse God's temple. The resurrection is the sign that Jesus has the authority to cleanse the temple. Only God has the right to cleanse the temple. Only God has the power to conquer death.

The resurrection is the last sign John mentions to bring us to faith. Jesus had been obliquely claiming to be God. This claim was to be vindicated when he rose from the dead. The signs were recorded by John so that we may believe that Jesus is the Christ, the Son of God (John 20v30–31).

A miraculous haul of fish

I think that the sign of the miraculous catch of one hundred and fifty-three fish, described in John 21, is a postscript to do with Peter's new vocation. Jesus called him to make and pastor disciples. He had gone back to his old trade of fishing, the trade he loved and with which he was comfortable. Jesus calls him to forsake this and follow him. For this reason I think that Jesus's question, *'Do you love me more than these?' (John 21v15),* could be a reference to the fish and not to the other disciples. Jesus has demonstrated that Peter need not worry about where the next meal was coming from, for Jesus had breakfast ready for the disciples. He would provide for their needs (Matthew 6v31–33).

So, interestingly, we have two bookends placed together in John 2, namely, the first and last signs to bring us to faith. The first sign was the turning of water into wine that Jesus had performed at the wedding in Cana, in Galilee. It should not surprise us that the resurrection is the last – the pinnacle of these signs. In John 2 we are also being shown that Jesus is our creator, redeemer and judge.

JESUS, OUR RULER AND JUDGE

When Jesus cleansed the temple the Jews demanded to know what right or authority he had for doing so. The same question was put to Moses when he tried to reconcile two Hebrew men: *'Who made you a ruler and judge over us?' (Acts 7v27, 35).* The resurrection of Jesus plainly points to the fact that he is our ruler and judge, and we shall give our account to him when we face him at the judgement. His resurrection from the dead guarantees this. His resurrection showed that he had the right to cleanse the temple! The Jews had questioned his right, and he responded by saying that if they destroyed the temple, that is, his body, he would raise it back to life, which he did.

His claim that God was his Father is vindicated, and his claim that judgement is given to the Son is proved. He has kept his word (John 2v19, John10v17–18) and he can be trusted.

He has conquered death.

WHAT IS OUR VERDICT?

Up to this point we have been weighing the evidence that John has been bringing before us. We have also considered other biblical evidence.

Now it is time for us to reach our verdicts.

- Who do we say Jesus is?
- Do we believe that Jesus is the Son of God?
- Do we believe that by believing in Jesus – that he is the Son of God, and that his death has paid the penalty for our sin – we may have eternal life?

The purpose of believing John's evidence is that we may have eternal life.

Would you like to receive God's gift of eternal life?

If you believe this Gospel, here is a prayer which you can pray in your heart to God, just where you are right now.

Heavenly Father, I have sinned against you, and I am truly sorry for my sins. Wash away all my sins by Jesus's blood. I acknowledge that Jesus is your one and only Son. I now invite Jesus to live in my heart as my Lord and Saviour. I welcome your Holy Spirit. As best as I know how, I give you my life. In Jesus's name. Amen.

(This prayer is adapted from R.T. Kendall's tract, *Can You Know for Certain That You Will go to Heaven When You Die?* Westminster Chapel, 1986.)

Chapter Nine

Who is Jesus? The Testimony of Moses

WHO IS MOSES?

Moses was a prophet raised up by God to lead God's chosen people out of slavery in Egypt and into the land that God had promised to them. He was a priest representing the people before God, and declaring God's Word to God's people. He recorded for us the essential early history of the world, and God's dealings with his people and humanity in general. Moses, inspired by the Holy Spirit, wrote the first five books of the Bible, namely Genesis, Exodus, Leviticus, Numbers and Deuteronomy.

These five books taken together could be described as the testimony of Moses.

Moses was born in terrible times for the Hebrews. Pharaoh, the king of Egypt, had just issued an edict that all Hebrew baby boys be killed. Moses's mother, however, placed him in a waterproof basket among the reeds at the river bank in an attempt to preserve his life. Pharaoh's daughter found Moses there, and she adopted him and brought him up at the palace. He was instructed in all the wisdom of the Egyptians (Acts 7v22). Moses later rejected this privileged lifestyle in order to identify with his own people and deliver them from the tyranny of slavery under the Egyptians. However, his own people rejected his rule, and he fled and became an exile in the land of Midian. After forty years God called him and sent him back to Egypt to deliver his people.

WHY IS THE TESTIMONY OF MOSES IMPORTANT?

In John 5v39 Jesus points out to the Jews that although they study the scriptures to find eternal life, and it is these very scriptures that bear witness to him, they refuse to seek eternal life from him. He then says that if they believed Moses they would also believe him, because Moses had written about him (John 5v46).

Moses testified to Jesus! How, you may wonder, did he do that? He was a prophet and foretold what Jesus would do, and why. Prophets would foretell what God would do, and sometimes they would also enact what God would do. Such acting could be costly, and involve much suffering for the prophet. For instance, Jonah had to enact drowning to show that the death of one man would appease the wrath of God, and that through Jonah's death many were saved from death. Jonah also enacted the resurrection of Jesus from the dead when the whale vomited Jonah onto dry land (Jonah 2v10).

Jesus gives a salutary warning when he recounts the story of the rich man and Lazarus (Luke16v19–31). In this story the rich man, who has died, pleads with Abraham to send

Lazarus to warn his five brothers lest they too end up in this place of torment, as he himself had.

Let us pay careful attention to Abraham's reply. He tells the rich man that his brothers have available to them the holy scriptures delivered to them by Moses and the prophets through the Holy Spirit. They are therefore without excuse if they disregard the scriptures and end up in torment. Abraham adds that even if the rich man's request were to be granted and someone were to rise from the dead to warn them, they would still not believe. The proof, says Abraham, is in how they treat God's Word.

Today we have Moses and the prophets freely available to us in our own language. We also have the New Testament. We will have no excuse when we stand before God and he asks us, 'Why did you reject my Son, Jesus? Why did you refuse the means of salvation that I provided for you?'

If we do not believe the Word of God, then signs, wonders and miracles will not convince us. I will return to the rich man and Lazarus in the concluding chapter.

Jesus expounds Moses and the prophets

Two disciples of Jesus were walking from Jerusalem to Emmaus, discussing recent events relating to Jesus. They discussed his life and death, and also the reports that some women of their company had seen him alive (Luke 24). Jesus joined them on their journey, but they were kept from recognising him. When they tell him what they have been discussing, he rebukes them for their unbelief because they had dismissed the women's testimony that Jesus was alive. See how he puts it in Luke 24v25–27: '... *O foolish men, and slow of heart to believe all that the prophets have spoken! Was it not necessary that the Christ should suffer these things and enter into his glory?' And beginning with Moses and all the prophets, he interpreted to them in all the scriptures the things concerning himself.*

The truth about Jesus was written beforehand in the Old Testament by Moses and all the prophets. This is why the testimony of Moses is important. This is why the Old Testament is important. This is why we ignore the Old Testament at our peril. This is why many Christians are impoverished by treating the Old Testament with scorn, or ignoring it altogether. Jesus affirmed the Old Testament. Moses identified the one whom the people of Israel were to look for.

John 1v45 states: *Philip found Nathanael, and said to him, 'We have found him of whom Moses in the law and also the prophets wrote, Jesus of Nazareth, the son of Joseph.'*

KEY EVENTS IN MOSES'S TESTIMONY

Let us now turn our attention to some of the key events in the testimony of Moses.

The early history of mankind

The first major events are described in the early chapters of Genesis, beginning with the creation of the world, and the rest of creation, with man set apart as the pinnacle of God's creation. This is followed by man's disobedience to God in the Garden of Eden, and its consequences. We have covered the Fall in chapter 2 (The Origin Of Death). Moses explains how and why death entered the world. He also introduces us to the solution to our problem of sin when he says that the seed of the woman shall bruise Satan's head and Satan shall, in turn, bruise his heel (Genesis 3v15). The seed of the woman refers to Jesus Christ. This is the first promise of the coming Messiah who will deliver us from the power that Satan has over us through death. He will do so by destroying death through his own death (Hebrews 2v14–15).

We see here that in the Garden of Eden, before there were Jews and Gentiles, God made this wonderful first promise of the coming Messiah to our ancestors. We are given a strong clue as to how the human race would be redeemed when we read that God killed an animal to clothe Adam and Eve suitably. They were clothed by God (Genesis 3v21). Their man-made aprons were not suitable, for they hid nothing from God's sight. The skins worked to cover their sins. They showed that blood had to be shed for there to be forgiveness of sin, and that God had to do the sacrificing – not man – for it to be effective (Hebrews 9v22).

The sacrifice of an animal and the shedding of its blood points to the sacrifice of Christ as the only way for our sins to be forgiven. Animal sacrifice in itself has no value but points to Christ's sacrifice. It is impossible, says Paul, for the blood of bulls and goats to take away sins (Hebrews 10v4). This is where the rule of 'an eye for an eye and a tooth for a tooth' has to be applied. The penalty for sin is human blood – not animal blood – because the blood of animals does not have the same value as human blood. Moreover, the blood must come from a sinless human. Only Christ's blood meets both criteria, for he was a sinless man.

Abel's sacrifice points to the Lamb of God

The next significant event we come to is the murder of Abel by his brother Cain. These two brothers were children of Adam and Eve. Abel knew what God wanted, and he obeyed by sacrificing a lamb. Cain, on the other hand, was determined to do better than his brother. He was a tiller of the soil – a horticulturalist. His offering of crops was rejected because he had rejected what God said he wanted, that is, an animal sacrifice. Adam and Eve would have explained to Cain and Abel the kind of sacrifice God required. They would have told them how God had sacrificed an animal and then clothed them with the skins.

Cain gets angry, and we can imagine what is going through his mind. He perhaps thinks to himself, 'All my hard work is not good enough, God? You want blood? I'll give you a blood sacrifice, if it's blood you want!' (1 John 3v11–12). Thus he murdered his righteous brother Abel because Abel's righteousness had exposed his own sinfulness. Abel had believed his parents' testimony that God demands the blood of a lamb to atone for sin, and so he sacrificed a lamb. In doing so he exposed the wicked-ness of Cain, for Cain did not accept God's Word and had chosen instead his own method of atonement, that is, his own works – his produce from the ground. His wickedness was unbelief. The faith of Abel exposed Cain's unbelief so he tried to silence the testimony of Abel. He demonstrated utter contempt for God.

However, God challenges Cain with a question: '…*What have you done? The voice of your brother's blood is crying to me from the ground' (Genesis 4v10).* Abel's blood was crying out for justice – for revenge. It is possible that the ground was soaked with Abel's blood, or that Cain had buried Abel's body in an attempt to hide the murder from his parents and from God. Nevertheless God heard the blood of Abel crying out for justice.

In contrast, when the blood of Jesus was shed on the cross, his blood cried out for mercy for us. *And to Jesus, the mediator of a new covenant, and to the sprinkled blood that speaks more graciously than the blood of Abel (Hebrews 12v24).*

And Jesus said, 'Father, forgive them; for they do not know what they do' (Luke 23v34).

Rejection is not pleasant. It can make us seethe with anger, especially if our best efforts are rejected. However, this helps us to understand, to some extent, how God feels about rejection. When Cain offered his sacrifice of produce from the ground instead of a lamb, he was rejecting what God had desired and ordained. Furthermore, he was rejecting the Word of God.

We need to learn from this. Those who put their faith in the sacrifice of Christ on the cross will, like Abel, be hated. They will be despised, persecuted, and perhaps even killed for their faith.

Noah points to the 'Ark' of Christ

Genesis 6 describes how terrible life on earth was in the days of Noah. God was grieved by what he had made because man had become wicked and rebellious. The thoughts of man's heart were also continually wicked. God therefore decided to blot out man and all creatures living on earth and in the air. However one man, Noah, found favour in God's sight, for he was righteous and walked with God. Here was a man who had fellowship with God.

God planned to destroy the earth with a flood, and told Noah to build an ark so that he and his family could escape the consequences of the flood. Noah built the ark in accordance with God's specifications. Noah was a preacher, and warned people of the judgement of God.

As word got round, people would come and gaze at this extraordinary construction that Noah was working on. They came to deride him, but he would take the opportunity to explain what he was doing, and why. He would urge them to repent. In 2 Peter 2v5 Noah is called a 'herald of righteousness': *By faith Noah, being warned by God concerning events as yet unseen, took heed and constructed an ark for the saving of his household; by this he condemned the world and became an heir of the righteousness which comes by faith (Hebrews 11v7).*

So what is our reaction to this historical account? Do we think it is fiction? Do we think that the flood never took place? Let us consider what we have been told:

- God was grieved by the depth of mankind's depravity;
- God warned mankind of the coming flood;
- God provided the way of escape – the ark;
- God saved through the ark those who trusted his Word;
- Faith was demonstrated by entering the ark;
- God judged mankind.

The ark is a type of Christ. It is a prophetic picture of how the world will be saved from God's judgement. The flood is a historic event that predicts the coming final judgement, and points to how we may be saved from judgement. *For as in Adam all die, so also in Christ shall all be made alive (1 Corinthians 15v22).* To be saved from the judgement of God we have to put our trust in his Son, Jesus Christ, alone. This is how we become 'in Christ'.

So where do we stand?

- Man is sinful: ... *all have sinned and fall short of the glory of God ... (Romans 3v23).*
- God will judge the world. He warns us of this in the Bible.
- He provides the way of escape. Jesus said: *'I am the way ...' (John 14v6).*

Do we believe that the work of Christ can save us?

Faith means putting our trust in Christ alone for salvation.

Abraham's word 'God will provide a lamb' points to Jesus

Abraham was a pagan who lived in Ur of the Chaldees, serving false gods (Joshua 24v2). God told Abraham to leave his home and go to a far-off country, and promised to give him land and many descendants. Abraham believed God's promise and went as instructed. God 'counted Abraham as righteous' because he believed the promise. He demonstrated his faith by setting out for the promised land. God had promised Abraham that he would have descendants 'as numerous as the sands of the sea'. His wife was barren, but he believed God's Word. When he was one hundred years old God gave him a son by his wife Sarah, who was ninety. He named his son Isaac.

Now Abraham became a prophet (Genesis 20v7), and was called by God to enact how God would save the world. God tells Abraham to sacrifice his only son, Isaac (Genesis 22v1–14). Abraham obeys and takes Isaac on a journey to the place of sacrifice on one of the mountains in the land of Moriah. On the way there Isaac asks his father, 'Where is the lamb for sacrifice?' How painful this question must have been to Abraham! Abraham's expectation was that God would provide a lamb, and if not, God would raise Isaac from the dead (Hebrews 11v17–19). He replied that God would provide the lamb. When Abraham was about to execute Isaac an angel called out to him to stop, and he obeyed. Looking up, he saw a ram that God had provided, caught in a bush. So he offered up the ram instead of Isaac.

This graphic account involving Isaac tells us that God will provide the substitutionary sacrifice, a lamb.

God would one day offer his own Son as a sacrifice to save the world. This is why John the Baptist announces Jesus with the words: '*Behold, the Lamb of God, who takes away the sin of the world!*' (*John 1v29*).

Joseph points to the world's need of Jesus as Saviour

Joseph, the son of Jacob, came from a large family and was gifted. In particular, he had the gift of dreams and of interpreting them. On the other hand he was also exceedingly proud and insensitive. He was Jacob's favourite, and his envious brothers hated him so much that they plotted to kill him. However, in the end, they sold him into slavery, and he became a slave in Egypt in the house of Potiphar, who was the captain of Pharaoh's guard. Potiphar entrusted Joseph with managing his house. However, one day, Joseph was falsely accused of attempted rape by Potiphar's wife, and imprisoned (Genesis 39).

Some years later God gave Pharaoh, king of Egypt, two dreams which no one could interpret except Joseph. The dreams were a warning from God that there would be seven years of plentiful harvests followed by seven years of famine.

God had arranged it in order to carry out his purpose for Israel. Joseph interpreted the dreams for Pharaoh and, furthermore, advised him what to do. Pharaoh appointed Joseph as Governor of Egypt and also manager of his household (Genesis 41).

We see that it was God who brought this about. During a severe worldwide famine, Joseph's brothers had to come to him for food not knowing, at first, who he was. God had sent Joseph on ahead to save his people. Joseph provided grain for Israel and for Egypt; moreover, all the earth came to Joseph for grain because the famine was worldwide, and there was nowhere else to go. If people did not go to Joseph, they perished.

God fixed it, and God still fixes it. The whole world must come to Christ for salvation. Why? Because salvation is found in no one else. We can go anywhere else we like, but we just will not be saved – that is, saved from the judgement of God.

Man-made religion is oppressive and seeks to control, but God always gives freedom (John 8v32, 36). We are free when we do that for which we were created. We were created to serve God. That is perfect freedom. When we are not serving God we are in bondage. Four hundred years later God said to another Pharaoh, *'Let my people go, that they may serve me ...' (Exodus 7v16)*. The freedom of the people of Israel came through the sacrifice of a lamb during the Passover, which in turn pointed to Christ, who died on a cross just over two thousand years ago, and by whose death we are redeemed – that is, set free to serve him.

Are we in bondage to religion? Have we been kept from serving the true God by human philosophy or ideology? Do we trust those who say that there is no God to answer to? Do we think that our baptism, going to church, or good works will earn us a place in heaven? They will not.

Are we in bondage to a particular lifestyle which we would prefer to hold on to, even though it may cost us eternal life and send us to hell?

God has been good to you and to me. Our gifts are from God. Everything we have is from God. Sometimes God has to get our attention because he wants to bless us, but in our ignorance we do not seek him. Since he loves us he may not give us everything we want. His love for us is great, and he is prepared to be misunderstood. He may even hurt us in order to bless us.

> 'Turn to me and be saved, all the ends of the earth! For I am God, and there is no other' (Isaiah 45v22). And there is salvation in no one else, for there is no other name under heaven given among men by which we must be saved (Acts 4v12).

> I will greatly rejoice in the LORD, my soul shall exult in my God; for he has clothed me with the garments of salvation, he has covered me with the robe of righteousness, as a bridegroom decks himself with a garland, and as a bride adorns herself with her jewels (Isaiah 61v10).

The cross of Christ is the glory of Christ. He gave his life freely and willingly, and the Father, God his heavenly Father, and ours, loves him for this (John 10v15–18). Can you imagine what it cost the Father to allow his only Son to go to the cross to bear our sins, and to have to turn his back on his beloved Son?

The Passover foreshadows the crucifixion of Jesus

The account of the Passover is found in Exodus 12. God, through Moses, had performed signs and wonders in Egypt, but God hardened Pharaoh's heart each time so that he refused to allow the Israelites to go and worship God in the wilderness (Exodus 10v1–2). Towards the end of these signs and wonders Pharaoh was trying to negotiate with God, seeking a compromise which, humanly speaking, was reasonable. The Israelites provided Pharaoh with a cheap labour force, and by not letting their children go, Pharaoh had a hold over the Israelites to ensure that they returned to serve him. But God's destiny for his people, all of them, was the Promised Land. God does not compromise; consider his commandment: *'You shall have no other gods before me'* *(Exodus 20v3).*

However, the last sign in Egypt – the killing of the firstborn of both man and beast – forced Pharaoh to drive the Israelites out of Egypt. An angel of the Lord smote the firstborn but bypassed the houses where God's people dwelt, sparing their firstborn, provided that the household had followed God's instruction on the Passover. The instruction was that each household had to slaughter a lamb and apply the blood to their doorposts. They had to roast the lamb and eat it. This latter command applied to the entire household, whereas the blood on the doorposts was to prevent the angel of death from slaying the firstborn.

All this required faith, believing what God had said, and doing it no matter how foolish it might have appeared. They had to believe what God had said through Moses, that the angel of death would pass through the land and kill all the firstborn in the land of Egypt.

By faith they had to apply the blood to the doorposts, and when they ate the lamb they identified with the lamb and partook of it. The people of Israel demonstrated their faith by literally sprinkling the blood on their doorposts and eating the lambs that they had slaughtered.

The Passover lamb pointed to Christ, who is our true Passover Lamb. We are required to drink his blood and eat his flesh (John 6v53–58), but not literally. We cannot do this literally. It is not how Jesus meant his words to be taken. They are meant to be taken in the same way as the concepts of the new birth, and being born again. The new birth is spiritual, not physical (John 3v3–6).

Thus eating Christ's flesh and drinking his blood means that we are required to believe Christ's words. This is how we partake of Christ. This is how we show faith.

The people of Israel were set free from slavery in Egypt. By faith we can be set free from sin: its penalty, its power, and finally its presence. Exodus 19v6 tells us that Israel was to be a nation of priests. A priest is one who represents man before God, and declares God's Word to man. So, Israel's role was to be priests to God on behalf of the world, that is, to represent themselves and the Gentiles before God. Priests had to eat the sacrifice. Hence we note that the people of Israel partook of these sacrificial lambs – the Passover lambs. A priest needs to partake of Jesus's flesh and blood (John 6v53–54). Passover can then be seen as enrolment to the priesthood. *But you are a chosen race, a royal priesthood, a holy nation, God's own people ... (1Peter 2v9–10).* This is known as the priesthood of all believers.

Once you put your trust in what Jesus, the Lamb of God, has done for you on the cross, you become a priest. Putting your trust in Christ is how you partake in his life and death.

It is by faith we do this, not by literally eating his flesh and drinking his blood. When Christ died on the cross for our sins, the curtain of the temple was torn in two from top to bottom (Matthew 27v51). God tore it, and this meant that Jesus had opened up the way for sinners to approach God directly. By faith in his death we are counted righteous before God. We can have direct access to God the Father because of what Jesus has done.

> *For by grace you have been saved, through faith; and this is not your own doing, it is the gift of God – not because of works, lest any man should boast (Ephesians 2v8–9).*

The snake on a pole points to Jesus on the cross

> *(4) From Mount Hor they set out by the way to the Red Sea, to go around the land of Edom; and the people became impatient on the way. (5) And the people spoke against God and against Moses, 'Why have you brought us up out of Egypt to die in the wilderness? For there is no food and no water, and we loathe this worthless food.' (6) Then the Lord sent fiery serpents among the people, and they bit the people, so that many people of Israel died. (7) And the people came to Moses, and said, 'We have sinned, for we have spoken against the Lord and against you; pray to the Lord, that he take away the serpents from us.' So Moses prayed for the people. (8) And the Lord said to Moses, 'Make a fiery serpent, and set it on a pole; and everyone who is bitten, when he sees it, shall live.' (9) So Moses made a bronze serpent, and set it on a pole; and if a serpent bit any man, he would look at the bronze serpent and live (Numbers 21v4–9).*

The background

The people of Israel had been slaves in Egypt for about four hundred years, as foretold by God when he spoke with Abraham (Genesis 15). Moses was sent by God to deliver Israel out of the hands of the Egyptians by performing signs and wonders in Egypt. This culminated in the Passover and the death of the firstborn man and beast in Egypt, except for the firstborn of the Israelites.

Now the people of Israel had liberty, and were on their way to the Promised Land. Were they happy, grateful and full of faith? No! They reacted badly when they were tried and tested with a variety of life-threatening situations, including a lack of food and drink. God provided them with food but they got bored with it. They even called the precious gift of food from God 'worthless'. How do we think that made God feel?

Here are some notes on the passage, followed by a summary:

- The people became impatient (v4);
- They spoke against God and Moses (v5);
- They accused God of bringing them out of Egypt to kill them in the wilderness (v5);
- They showed ingratitude (v5);
- They despised the miraculous gift of God: ... *we loathe this worthless food* (the manna in the wilderness provided by God: v5);
- God sent snakes among them (v6);
- Many Israelites were bitten and died (v6);
- The people acknowledged their sin and rebellion against God and Moses (v7);
- They pleaded with Moses to ask God to remove the snakes (v7);

- Moses prayed for the people (v7);
- God did not remove the snakes (v8);
- He gave his own remedy through Moses (v8);
- The remedy was in the form of the bronze serpent and was available to all (v8);
- The Israelites had to believe the promise and act as if they believed it, that is, demonstrate faith (v8). How? By turning their gaze to the bronze serpent lifted up on a pole (v8);
- One look was enough (v8);
- There was only one bronze serpent (v9).

Summary of passage

The Israelites were on the way from Egypt to Canaan and, as was their custom, they had rebelled against God. God had sent snakes in among them, and several Israelites died from snake bites. The remaining people begged Moses to pray to God to remove the snakes.

God told Moses to make a fiery serpent and hoist it high up on a pole so that whenever a snake bit an Israelite he was to look at the bronze serpent and, by just a look, live: '... *everyone who is bitten, when he sees it, shall live*' (*Numbers 21v8*).

We need to ask the question, 'Why didn't God just remove the snakes?' Surely that would have solved the problem. This is what the people had asked Moses to pray for. God did not grant their request, but provided his own solution. It was a solution that required faith. They had to believe his word that a look at the bronze serpent was sufficient to heal them. Here is a clue to our problem with suffering; in this instance it was an opportunity for faith.

The stark fact is that all of us will face death one day. We cannot avoid it. It should turn us to faith, to look to God for a solution – a lasting solution. God provides the solution; Jesus is God's solution to the problem of death. Jesus has conquered death.

Jesus himself recounts the snake incident in his discourse with Nicodemus (John 3v14–16): *And as Moses lifted up the serpent in the wilderness, so must the Son of man be lifted up, that whoever believes in him may have eternal life. For God so loved the world that he gave his only Son, that whoever believes in him should not perish but have eternal life.*

Jesus is explaining to Nicodemus what is going to happen on Good Friday. He is saying that if you want eternal life, you will only receive it if you believe that Jesus's death pays the penalty for your sin – your rebellion against God. What Jesus said to Nicodemus is good news for all of us.

There are two ways into heaven:

- Through Jesus Christ;
- Through our own efforts to be good enough.

The problem with the second way is that the standard of attainment is impossible.

All have sinned and fall short of the glory of God (Romans 3v23). We are measured against Jesus Christ himself. None of us can live up to his standard. He was sinless. We cannot get to heaven through our own good works.

That leaves the first way, which is the only way. Jesus said, *'I am the way, and the truth, and the life; no one comes to the Father, but by me' (John 14v6).* The only way to have peace with God and obtain eternal life is through Jesus Christ.

Why is this so? God has ordained it this way so that his Son receives all the glory.

We have considered some aspects of the testimony of Moses, and have seen how God ordains the means of salvation on his own terms. The requirement is to trust God's Word. We have considered the following:

- God shed blood to clothe Adam and Eve;
- God accepted Abel's sacrifice of a lamb;
- God saved Noah through the ark;
- God provided Abraham with a lamb to sacrifice as a substitute for Isaac;
- God saved the world from famine through one man, Joseph;
- God passed over the Israelite homes when he saw the blood of the lamb;
- God provided the bronze serpent so that the Israelites might live;
- God has provided Jesus as the only way to save us from eternal damnation.

All of this points to the unique and exclusive means of salvation in Christ alone.

It does not matter one iota what others do or do not do. You have to answer for yourself when you stand before God. God has ordained it so; we would be foolish to seek any other means of salvation – for there isn't one.

Chapter Ten

The Exclusiveness of Jesus Christ

In this chapter we will look at the claim of Jesus Christ that the way to God is through him, and him alone: *'I am the way, and the truth, and the life; no one comes to the Father, but by me'* (*John 14v6*).

Two questions that we might ask come to mind:

- Is this true?
- If so, why has God made it so?

Jesus is clearly stating that if you want to live in the presence of God, you can only gain access through him. This claim is supported by Peter when he says, *'And there is salvation in no one else, for there is no other name under heaven given among men by which we must be saved'* (*Acts 4v12*).

You have to decide whether this claim is true, and then consider what to do about it. I cannot do that for you. I believe it is true, and will attempt to give you a reason for it being so.

The reason for it being true is entirely dependent on the identity of Jesus. His claim to be God's Son is at stake.

The Father judges no one, but has given all judgment to the Son, that all may honour the Son, even as they honour the Father. He who does not honour the Son does not honour the Father who sent him (John 5v22–23).

We see that God the Father desires to honour his only Son:

- God honours his Son by making him the judge (John 5v22–23).
- God honours his Son by making him the Saviour (Matthew 1v21).
- God honours his Son by making him priest (Hebrews 7v21).
- God honours his Son by making him king (Hebrews 1v8).

If you had wanted to be saved from the flood in Noah's day, you would have entered Noah's ark. Noah's ark was the means God provided to escape his judgement. In the ark, you would have life. Outside, you would die. No one listened to the preaching of Noah, and they suffered the consequences of the catastrophic flood. It rained all over the earth for forty days. The whole earth was flooded. It happened once, but it will never happen again. God has promised that he will never destroy the earth by water again. He even gives us a sign, the rainbow. When you see the rainbow, be reassured that God keeps his word (Genesis 9v11–16).

The ark of Noah is a graphic, prophetic illustration of Jesus Christ. Jesus Christ is our ark. If we enter him by faith we will not be damned.

His exclusiveness is shown when he washes the feet of the disciples. He gives Peter his exclusive terms of service in John 13v8. Peter wanted to serve Christ on his own terms: *'You shall never wash my feet.'* He is rebuked by Jesus, who tells him, *'If I do not wash you, you have no part in me.'*

This tells us that if we want to follow Jesus we have to do so on his terms, not ours. Peter was given a choice, with no compromise or consensus. Salvation is on Christ's terms alone, and no negotiation is possible.

Chapter Eleven

The Resurrection of Jesus

Why is it thought incredible by any of you that God raises the dead? (Acts 26v8).

THE RESURRECTION: ITS PREDICTION

We have already seen in John's Gospel that Jesus predicted his resurrection. He is quoted by John as saying, *'Destroy this temple, and in three days I will raise it up' (John 2v19–21).* Jesus was referring to his body when he spoke of 'this temple'.

Mark records three occasions when Jesus foretold his death and resurrection.

Mark 8v31: *...and be killed, and after three days rise again.*
Mark 9v31: *...and when he is killed, after three days he will rise.*
Mark 10v34: *...and kill him; and after three days he will rise.*

THE RESURRECTION: ITS OCCURRENCE

We have also considered the encounter that Mary Magdalene had with Jesus after he had risen from the dead. Here we will look at the words of Paul in the first letter to the Corinthians.

> *For I delivered to you as of first importance what I also received, that Christ died for our sins in accordance with the scriptures, that he was buried, that he was raised on the third day in accordance with the scriptures, and that he appeared to Cephas, then to the twelve. Then he appeared to more than five hundred brethren at one time, most of whom are still alive, though some have fallen asleep (1 Corinthians 15v3–6).*

Paul himself was a witness, for Christ appeared to him on a journey from Jerusalem to Damascus. Paul was converted as a result. He stopped persecuting Christians, and began to preach the very faith that he had been trying to eradicate (Acts 9v1–6; Galatians 1v22–23).

The appearance of Jesus to so many is important because so many of them were still alive when Paul wrote this letter; his statement concerning the resurrection could be verified by the eyewitnesses.

You will remember how Thomas, the man who would not believe the testimony of his fellow disciples without tangible evidence, had met Jesus and confessed him as *'My Lord and my God!' (John 20v28).*

Jesus had a physical body which, though he was now risen, retained the marks of his suffering. These scars were trophies of his glorious sacrifice, his total devotion to his Father in heaven and his love for us – the fallen race awaiting the judgement.

Paul is saying that these facts are of critical importance for us. He received all this from the risen Christ, whom he met on his journey to Damascus. The audacious preaching of Stephen at his trial had greatly disturbed Paul. At the time of Stephen's trial Paul had been known as Saul of Tarsus. Paul had come to learn the truth, and also how to defend himself in court, from Stephen. Stephen cared not for his own safety, so long as he could proclaim Christ. Jesus said: '... *unless a grain of wheat falls into the earth and dies, it remains alone; but if it dies, it bears much fruit' (John 12v24).* Stephen died, but was exceptionally fruitful after his death through the ministry of Paul. However, it is God who converted Paul when he met Jesus, when he was on his way to Damascus to persecute Christians! This is why anti-conversion laws are futile. No man ever converts another. Only God converts, and no one can stop God.

What are the vital facts?

- Christ has died;
- Christ was buried;
- Christ is risen;
- Christ was seen alive.

Christ died for our sins. This is why God became man. The angel declared to Joseph that his virgin bride-to-be would bear a son: '... *she will bear a son, and you shall call his name Jesus, for he will save his people from their sins' (Matthew 1v21).*

But God shows his love for us in that while we were yet sinners Christ died for us (Romans 5v8).

Some deny that Jesus died. In 1 Corinthians 15 Paul is arguing the case for the resurrection of Jesus, and says that if Christ did not rise from the dead then our faith is futile, and we are even found to be misrepresenting God, which is a form of blasphemy. He argues strongly that Christ has been raised from the dead. Clearly, if Christ is raised, he had to die first.

THE BURIAL OF JESUS

> For I delivered to you as of first importance what I also received, that Christ died for our sins in accordance with the scriptures, that he was buried, that he was raised on the third day in accordance with the scriptures, and that he appeared to Cephas, then to the twelve (1 Corinthians 15v3–5).

Cephas is another name for Peter (John 1v42). The reference to 'the twelve' does not include Judas Iscariot, who hanged himself and was replaced (Acts 1v15–26). His replacement had to be someone who had witnessed the resurrection.

We should note here how 1Corinthians 15v3–4 tells us that the burial of Jesus was of first importance. Often we focus on the death and resurrection, but Paul includes the burial of Jesus as a fact of primary importance. He gives it equal weight to Jesus's death and resurrection. There were more than five hundred eyewitnesses, most of whom were alive when Paul wrote this letter (1 Corinthians 15v6).

So why is the burial of Jesus so important? Is it merely to show that he was dead? What does it add to state that Jesus was buried?

The main reason he was buried was that he had to 'fulfil all righteousness'. This phrase occurs in the account of Jesus's

122

baptism in Matthew 3v13–17. John the Baptist was ready to refuse to baptise Jesus, but he later agreed when Jesus told him that *it was necessary to fulfil all righteousness*. So, at his baptism, Jesus was buried, figuratively speaking, by John the Baptist, in the river Jordan.

Jesus was buried by Joseph of Arimathea, who was a rich man (Matthew 27v57), with the help of Nicodemus. They were members of the council, and therefore prominent Jews, who had been secret followers of Jesus. They risked their all, their reputation, career, social standing, indeed their very lives, by openly associating themselves with the corpse of this despised and rejected man. Nicodemus had already tasted this suffering when pleading with the council not to pre-judge Jesus (John 7v48–52).

When Jesus was dead the law was fulfilled, for he was buried on the same day that he died, as required by the law. For the law says: … *if a man has committed a crime punishable by death and he is put to death, and you hang him on a tree, his body shall not remain all night upon the tree, but you shall bury him the same day, for a hanged man is accursed by God; you shall not defile your land which the Lord your God gives you for an inheritance (Deuteronomy 21v22–23).*

Christ did not come to abolish the law but to fulfil it. So here we have two burials, one at each end of his ministry, the first being his baptism. The law demanded that Jesus be buried the very day he died, for he had been hung on a tree, a crudely made wooden cross. So even in death he had fulfilled the law.

These two members of the council must have exercised their minds greatly all day concerning Jesus's crucifixion and, in all probability, they did so separately, only coming together when Joseph had summoned up the courage to go to Pilate and ask for the body of Jesus. We cannot underestimate the courage of this secret believer, for it was hardly the time to identify with Jesus. Jesus's closest disciples had deserted him, and Peter later denied Jesus three times before the cock crowed, just as Jesus had predicted.

The courage of Joseph and Nicodemus is not without precedent. The valiant men of Jabesh Gilead had rescued the body of King Saul from the victorious Philistines and had given him a decent burial. They had risked their lives for a corpse – the corpse of their king (1 Samuel 31v8–13). Rizpah, the daughter of Aiah, covered the bodies of the seven sons of Saul and kept watch over them during the barley harvest (2 Samuel 21v10). She kept the birds of the air from eating their flesh by day, and kept the beasts of the field away by night. She was a courageous woman who honoured these seven sons of King Saul, two of whom were also her sons.

We also read of the disciples of John the Baptist risking their lives to bury his body after John had been beheaded by King Herod (Mark 6v29). Devout men risked their lives to bury Stephen (Acts 8v2).

So here we can consider the work of Joseph of Arimathea. He wanted to protect Jesus's body from further dishonour and humiliation by scavengers. He could not bear the thought of Jesus being humiliated in death as a trophy for the Gentiles who would mock, 'See now the King of the Jews!' So they had to take him down. You may remember that a Roman soldier had already thrust a spear through Jesus's side, perhaps for sport. They also spat on him and mocked him with a cruel and savage crown of thorns which had torn into his scalp.

The burial had to be carried out quickly because the Sabbath was close (Mark 15v42–43; John 19v31–34, 42), and Joseph had his own brand-new tomb close to hand which he made available for the burial. The convenience of this was important, but it may also have crossed his mind that he would be buried later in the same tomb as Jesus (1 Kings 13v30–32). If they wanted to bury Jesus they had to make a quick decision and proceed with much haste.

They used an extraordinarily large quantity of spices for his burial (100lb/45kg) which would have been very expensive. This extravagance indicates that his followers had recognised Jesus as king. Pilate had correctly called Jesus 'The King of the Jews', although he was being sarcastic.

Jesus was buried in haste on the same day because he was accursed for our sakes. *Christ redeemed us from the curse of the law, having become a curse for us – for it is written, 'Cursed be everyone who hangs on a tree' (Galatians 3v13).*

Jesus was charged with blasphemy and the penalty for blasphemy was death by stoning. If he had been stoned, then you could say that he was not cursed, and did not bear the curse for man. The fact is that he was crucified: he was hung by nails from a tree, and therefore 'cursed'.

Joseph and Nicodemus not only risked publicly identifying themselves with Jesus, but also had to contend with two other problems.

Joseph went to Pilate. Pilate was a Gentile, and therefore seen by the Jews as unclean.

Peter explained the law when God told him to visit Cornelius, a Roman centurion: *You yourselves know how unlawful it is for a Jew to associate with or to visit any one of another nation; but God has shown me that I should not call any man common or unclean (Acts 10v28).*

The second problem was that handling a dead body would make them unclean, but they also knew that a 'hanged' body had to be buried that same day (Deuteronomy 21v22–23).

The burial of Jesus does not prove his death; it confirms it. Pilate had certified his death before he released the body to Joseph. The Jews certainly knew he was dead; that is why they placed a guard at the tomb, lest his disciples steal the body and claim that he had risen.

The burial was to fulfil all righteousness by Jesus in his death. This is important, for Christ not only paid the penalty for our sins but he fulfilled all righteousness on our behalf. He did this completely.

His burial also fulfilled the prophecy of Isaiah:

> *And they made his grave with the wicked and with a rich man in his death ... (Isaiah 53v9).*

THE RESURRECTION: ITS MEANING AND SIGNIFICANCE

We have been looking into Paul's statement about what is important in the Christian faith, that is, the key elements of doctrine. We have considered Christ's death and his burial. It was necessary to take a detour because Paul has given weight to these elements. Now, however, it is time to return to the resurrection and consider its meaning. Some deny it, while others say that it was not a literal bodily resurrection.

Let us pay close attention, and we will see the importance of the resurrection in the lives of us all. It is the glory of Christ. God the Father is glorified by the resurrection of

Jesus Christ. If Christ did not die then there is no resurrection, and if there is no resurrection then we are all doomed and have no escape from eternal damnation.

Jesus said, *'For this reason the Father loves me, because I lay down my life, that I may take it again. No one takes it from me, but I lay it down of my own accord. I have power to lay it down, and I have power to take it again; this charge I have received from my Father'* (John 10v17–18).

So, if Jesus did not die or if he did not rise from the dead, then he is lying, and his claim to be God is false. This is why the resurrection is important: it tells us about Jesus; it verifies his identity. He is the good shepherd who laid down his life for the sheep (John 10v11).

Acts 17v30–31 tells us that the resurrection of Jesus is our guarantee that we will face God and be judged.

Christ has conquered death for us so that we can be certain of victory over death, provided we have put our faith in him.

The Holy Spirit vindicates Jesus Christ through his resurrection from the dead (Romans 1v3–4). The Holy Spirit bears witness to the identity of Jesus Christ, and to his power and authority. To reject the testimony of the Holy Spirit, who gives full glory to Jesus Christ, is blaspheming the Holy Spirit. It is the only sin that can keep you out of heaven (Mark 3v28–30).

John states that the resurrection fulfils scripture, that is the Old Testament, and also the Word Jesus had spoken (John 2v18–22). Peter's sermon on the day of Pentecost gives us further information. Peter quotes Psalm 16v10 and explains that King David, who was a prophet, was prophesying about the resurrection of the Christ (Acts 2v29–31).

The resurrection fulfils Christ's very Word (John 2v18–20). God does not lie. So, if Jesus did not rise from the dead, then we must conclude that he was a liar, and that he was not the Christ, the Son of God. Furthermore, since King David prophesied that the Christ would rise from the dead, then if Jesus of Nazareth did not rise from the dead we must wait for another Christ who will die for our sins and rise from the dead, for this is what the Old Testament asserts.

1 Corinthians 15 gives several reasons for the importance of the resurrection from the dead, e.g. *If Christ has not been raised, your faith is futile and you are still in your sins (1 Corinthians 15v17).* The dire consequences of such a situation, that is, eternal damnation, do not bear considering.

Chapter Twelve

Conclusion

In the introduction to this book we considered briefly the notion of conducting our own funeral, and what we would say to the gathered people. This question originally arose in my mind when my grandfather died in 1981. As we travelled to the church in the funeral cortège I wondered whether he had gone to heaven or hell. There was no way of finding out. He had been a faithful church attender all his life, but then so were my brother and I. Our attendance at church did not make us Christians, nor did our baptism as infants. Both of us came to put our trust in Jesus for salvation when we were students living away from home. My brother and I had tried to talk to our grandfather about the gospel for several years after our conversions, but this proved very difficult because he had become deaf. Although he wore hearing aids he was reluctant to switch them on. Neither of us ever had the common sense to write to him. When he died we stopped praying for him. It was now too late for him to put his trust in Jesus if he had not done so in his lifetime. Nothing would change his eternal destiny now. It was fixed. So where did he go? We do not know. However, the account of the thief on the cross allows us to hope that we may see him again one day.

Let us now consider one of the thieves who was crucified with Jesus. The two thieves hung on crosses either side of Jesus. One of them prayed to Jesus while hanging on a cross. Here, indeed, was a 'death-bed conversion'. He and the other thief had initially reviled Jesus (Matthew 27v44). He later rebuked the other thief, who had taunted Jesus: *'Are you not the Christ? Save yourself and us!' (Luke 23v39).* He acknowledges that Jesus has done nothing wrong, whilst they were being justly punished for their wrong deeds. He had come to fear God and was now concerned with his eternal destiny. He prayed for salvation at the last moment thus: *'Jesus, remember me when you come into your kingdom' (Luke 23v42).*

His prayer was answered immediately when Jesus replied: *'Today you will be with me in Paradise' (Luke 23v43).*

This is prayer. Answered prayer!

Prayer is talking to Jesus without the need of a go-between, that is, a priest, a saint, or Mary.

It is not exactly the most articulate sinner's prayer, but it is a heartfelt and desperate plea.

And it was effective. His prayer was answered!

Now consider this notion about the man, somewhat fanciful perhaps, but based on the known experiences of families over the years: his parents were possibly respectable members of the Jewish community who had done their best to bring up their son, but he turned out to be a thief. He had brought shame on the family name. They had longed for his repentance, for his going straight and turning to God, but now he has been tried justly, and crucified. Their prayers and longings seemingly unanswered, they have given up on him. However, they do not see what takes place between their son and Jesus in those dying moments. Neither do we see what takes place in someone's heart at the end of their life. We can only warn and plead with people to turn to Jesus while they live, and then we must leave the matter with Jesus.

The point is that we cannot know whether people will end up in heaven or hell, but we can be sure that wherever they end up they would want to plead one message if they could speak at their own funeral.

How can we be sure? Let us now return to the story Jesus relates about the rich man and Lazarus in Luke 16.

We learn from this account that the rich man had lived for the here and now, and had not been bothered by the prospect of death or what would happen after he died. He had lived for pleasure, and had no regard for Moses and the prophets. Perhaps he had a beautiful leather-bound Old Testament in pristine condition which had pride of place on his bookshelf. Inside this tome were the words of Moses and the prophets. We have examined the testimony of Moses in chapter 9.

The rich man is keenly aware that his brothers also hold no regard for the words of Moses and the prophets. This is why he wants Abraham to send Lazarus back to them. The brothers all knew the beggar Lazarus, for he sat at the rich man's gate. They could not really miss him when they visited for Sunday lunch. They knew he had died. So, were he to come back, they would give heed to his warnings, or so the rich man thought. He thought a miracle would convince them. He was desperate for them not to join him in the place of torment.

However, we are told that this would not be the case. Since they rejected Moses and the prophets, says Abraham, they would not be convinced if someone should rise from the dead.

Jesus himself said to the Jews that if they did not hear Moses then they would not believe his own words (John 5v45–47).

We should note here that when Jesus raised his friend, Lazarus, from the dead many Jews believed in Jesus, but the chief priests then sought to put Lazarus to death as well as Jesus. They rejected Jesus in spite of the miracle which they could not deny.

Why are Moses and the prophets given such weight by Jesus? Because they bear witness to Jesus!

Let us consider two other accounts here: Judas, and the thief on the cross.

Did you notice that both men were thieves (John 12v6)?

We have seen in our brief look at the Ten Commandments that we are all thieves.

The thief on the cross shows us the way – the only way – of escape, which is to look to Jesus and ask for mercy (John 14v6; Acts 4v12; John 3v14–15).

The thief on the cross literally looked to Jesus for salvation. One look in faith to Jesus, the Son of God, saves us (John 3v14–15).

Now, the question is this: How shall we escape if we neglect so great a salvation?

We shall not!

There is no other way! (Acts 4v12). Jesus said, *'I am the way, and the truth, and the life; no one comes to the Father, but by me'* (*John 14v6*).

We have less excuse than the rich man and his family. They had Moses and the prophets, but we have so much more. We have both the Old and New Testaments.

THE WAY OF ESCAPE

> *Therefore we must pay the closer attention to what we have heard, lest we drift away from it. For if the message declared by angels was valid and every transgression or disobedience received a just retribution, how shall we escape if we neglect such a great salvation? It was declared at first by the Lord, and it was attested to us by those who heard him, while God also bore witness by signs and wonders and various miracles and by gifts of the Holy Spirit distributed according to his own will (Hebrews 2v1–4).*

There is no earthly reason why God should have revealed to you or me the simplest biblical truths in our own language. The fact is, it is written so plainly, and we simply condemn ourselves if we choose to ignore it. We will be judged on what we did with God's Word.

Did we ignore it?

Did we reject it?

Did we admire it as poetry and nothing more?

Did we put it on our bookshelf as some precious ornament?

Did we carry around that Gideon New Testament in a school blazer pocket like some sort of lucky charm, as the author did many years ago?

Were we put off by others misleading us as to its meaning, or by the hypocritical lives of some who call themselves Christians? Or by the genuine Christians who did not meet our expectations in the way they lived? Real Christians can let you down because we still have a sinful nature.

Ultimately, we ourselves are responsible for ourselves to God.

Is there no hope, no glimmer of light?

The way of escape is provided by God himself. We all suffer everyday temptations and trials (1 Corinthians 10v13). Right now, you may be facing a trial of hopelessness. But hope is found in the promises of God (2 Peter 1v3–4).

God's desire is that all people be saved. His desire is to save each one of us from eternal damnation (2 Peter 3v9).

I have attempted to show the way of escape in the preceding pages, so that you also may escape. How shall we escape, if we neglect this offer of so great a salvation?

Jesus Christ is the way of salvation. His death on the cross appeased the wrath of God. That wrath was directed our way, and justly so because of our sin – our unbelief.

Since Christ has paid the price of our sin, why on earth would anyone in their right mind spurn his gift of salvation and try to atone for their sin by their own efforts?

If we neglect Christ's salvation we will, without doubt, end up in hell. God has ordained that the only means of salvation is through his Son, Jesus Christ. He has done this so that all glory goes to Jesus. God arranges things so that his purposes will always be fulfilled. If we humble ourselves and seek salvation from Christ, then we must do so on his terms. This is non-negotiable. He alone has authority to forgive sins, for he is God.

If you have come to the point where you would like to receive God's gift of eternal life now, then please pray the prayer below. This prayer was included earlier in the book, but I have repeated it here for your convenience. In praying this prayer you will be acknowledging before God that you are a sinner, that you deserve the punishment Jesus took for us, and that your only hope for God's mercy is to put all your trust in Jesus's death on the cross for your sins. You will also be asking Jesus to be the Lord of your life from now on. Learning to live a life that pleases God is not the means of earning your salvation, for, as we have seen, salvation is the gift of God. Rather, having received the mercy of God, we will want to live our lives to please him out of sheer gratitude.

Heavenly Father, I have sinned against you and I am truly sorry for my sins. Wash away all my sins by Jesus's blood. I acknowledge that Jesus is your one and only Son. I now invite Jesus to live in my heart as my Lord and Saviour. I welcome your Holy Spirit. As best as I know how, I give you my life. In Jesus's name. Amen.

(This prayer is adapted from R.T. Kendall's tract, *Can You Know for Certain That You Will go to Heaven When You Die?*, Westminster Chapel, 1986.)

Appendix – A Family Funeral

I have included here the address that I gave at my sister's funeral in 2001. She died unexpectedly after being in great pain for several days. The cause was not diagnosed until she was rushed to hospital where she was found to have deep-vein thrombosis, but by then it was too late, and she died shortly after.

FAREWELL TO MOYNA: JUNE 2001

I remember two conversations I had with my sister Moyna. The first conversation took place three years ago, at my wedding. The minister had asked during his talk, 'Do you know for certain that if you were to die today you would go to heaven?' At the reception, Moyna's characteristically humorous response to me was, 'What if I had dropped dead on the spot when he asked that question?'

The second conversation took place about two weeks ago when I rang Moyna, and she asked me to pray for her. I agreed to pray for her but told her that she could also pray for herself. However, she felt that it was a bit of a cheek for her to ask God for anything, bearing in mind her previous attitude to God. So I told her about John Newton. He was formerly a blasphemer, and a slave-ship captain who had worked the slave-trade routes. During one of his voyages there was a great storm, and his ship was in danger of breaking up. It was then that he cried out to God for help, and God delivered him from the storm. As a result of this experience he became a Christian.

I explained to her that Newton, the former blasphemer, was the man who had written the hymn *How sweet the name of Jesus sounds*. Moyna then started talking about the hymns sung at Dad's funeral, mentioning *Amazing Grace*. I told her that this hymn had also been written by John Newton, which was quite a coincidence. Moyna's attitude to God had been softening gradually over time.

Luke says of Jesus: *He also told this parable to some who trusted in themselves that they were righteous and despised others: 'Two men went up into the temple to pray, one a Pharisee and the other a tax collector. ... But the tax collector, standing far off, would not even lift up his eyes to heaven, but beat his breast, saying, "God, be merciful to me a sinner!" I tell you, this man went down to his house justified, rather than the other; for every one who exalts himself will be humbled, but he who humbles himself will be exalted' (Luke 18v9–10, 13–14).*

Moyna did not consider herself worthy of prayer, showing humility and knowing her position before God. In spite of this she asked for prayer, hoping to find healing and mercy from him. Moyna indicated by this what has been called 'implicit faith'. For this reason I hope to see Moyna again, in heaven. We certainly prayed for Moyna to be healed. God can heal, and sometimes he does, but she died. We do not know why God did not heal her. We may never know.

What then should we do in response to a sudden death like Moyna's? Our first reaction may be to feel cheated. Moyna was a dear sister and a great friend, and ours is a great loss, but should we feel cheated? I would answer, 'No'.

We should respond in three ways.

Give thanks

He who brings thanksgiving as his sacrifice honours me; to him who orders his way aright I will show the salvation of God! (Psalm 50v23).

We should give thanks to God for allowing us the privilege of sharing the life of a wonderful person for so long. Just think of all the things you most enjoyed about that person, and say, 'Thank you, Jesus!' – even through your tears. A sacrifice, by definition, is costly and painful. To give thanks in this way honours God. Psalm 50v23 says so, and finishes with a promise: ... *I will show the salvation of God!* We should give thanks and ask God to give us his salvation, thus claiming the promise.

Take heed

Moyna's sudden death is not unusual. Death can come to us at any time, and when we are least expecting it.

This was the very point of the minister's question, 'Do you know for certain that if you were to die today, you would go to heaven?'

> *And he made from one every nation of men to live on all the face of the earth, having determined allotted periods and the boundaries of their habitation, that they should seek God, in the hope that they might feel after him and find him (Acts 17:26–27).*

Seek God now – don't wait!

Hebrews 9v27 tells us: ... *it is appointed to men to die once, and after that comes judgment ...*

We have only this life to seek God. We seek God through Jesus.

> *Jesus said to him, 'I am the way, and the truth, and the life; no one comes to the Father, but by me' (John 14v6).*

> *And there is salvation in no one else, for there is no other name under heaven given among men by which we must be saved (Acts 4v12).*

All of us can go to heaven when we die. The promise is given to each of us. Salvation is free. It is based not on what we do or how good or bad we might be, but on what God has done in sending his Son to die on a cross for our sins just over two thousand years ago. Jesus has paid the penalty for our sins. We do not need to pay the penalty. Jesus has paid it in full. Believe it, and ask God for his pardon for your sin on the basis of what Jesus Christ has done.

Lightning Source UK Ltd.
Milton Keynes UK
UKHW021810051218
333504UK00003B/174/P